RUGGED LAND | 401 WEST STREET · SECOND FLOOR · NEW YORK CITY · NY 10014 · USA

PAYTON

By Connie, Jarrett, and Brittney Payton

Other Titles by Connie Payton

STRONGER THAN CANCER

Other Titles by Walter Payton

NEVER DIE EASY
(with Don Yaeger)

SWEETNESS
(with Jerry B. Jenkins)

Dedication

With profound gratitude, Jarrett, Brittney and I dedicate this book to Walter Payton's beloved fans. You can never imagine how it warms our hearts that "34" is still proudly worn by so many men, women and children.

To those who continue to remember the man they called "Sweetness," this is for you.

The Payton Family

RuggedLand

Published by Rugged Land, LLC

401 WEST STREET · SECOND FLOOR · NEW YORK · NY · 10014 · USA

RUGGED LAND and colophon are trademarks of Rugged Land, LLC

PUBLISHER'S CATALOGING-IN-PUBLICATION DATA

Payton, Connie.
Payton
/ by Connie, Jarrett and Brittney Payton. - - 1st ed.

p. cm.

ISBN 1-59071-056-8

1. Payton, Walter, 1954-1999.
2. Football players—United States—Biography.
I. Payton, Jarrett.
II. Payton, Brittney.
III. Title.

GV939.P39P39 2005   796.332'092
QBI05-700256

Book Design by
JK Naughton Design

RUGGED LAND WEBSITE ADDRESS: WWW.RUGGEDLAND.COM

Table of Contents

FOREWORD

The Gamechanger

by Brett Favre

Walter Payton was from Mississippi. So am I. Growing up in that state during his NFL career, you had to be in awe of him. He had a huge impact on all of us. My two brothers and I shared a bedroom covered with football posters and memorabilia, most of it about Walter or the Bears' 1985 Super Bowl team.

There are lots of great players who've come out of Mississippi— Jerry Rice, Archie Manning. But I think you have to put Walter at the very top of that list. I played on several different teams throughout high school and college, and for all of the Mississippi youths that I played with, he was the icon, the idol. He set the pace for all of us. Even if you weren't a running back, Walter was still the guy you looked up to for how to be a team player and also just a good guy, on and off the field.

It's funny to think back. I can recall a lot of teammates doing their best to imitate Walter's running style. But if there was ever a playing style that you couldn't imitate, it was his. Nobody ever even got close to him. You could do your best to copy his moves, and if you were fast you could match him on speed; but this thing that you couldn't copy about Walter was his determination, his mental game. He just was not going to be tackled, he was not going to go down. Period. And it was all willpower and determination.

You can't remember what Walter's best plays were, because you saw him do the same impossible things so many times, over and over again. How many times can you remember him putting his head down and breaking through three huge guys on the tackle? How many times did we see him on third and goal jumping the whole defensive line for a touchdown? Walter was not the biggest, not the strongest and not the fastest, he just ran for the most yards. That says it all.

Obviously, as a quarterback I wasn't directly influenced by his playing style, but I can tell you what it means to have a running back like Walter Payton carrying the football for you. A guy with that kind of talent alters the whole face of the game. He shifts the dynamic of everything that's going on out on that field. He takes an enormous amount of pressure off of the quarterback. He gives you more control over the clock, more control over possession. A player like Walter isn't just a game saver, he's a gamechanger.

And he was a fighter, and a winner, right until the very end.

In November of 1999, a week after Walter died, the Chicago Bears played against me and the Packers. They dedicated the game to his memory. We knew they would be bringing a lot of heart and a lot of fight out onto the field, but, to be honest, we weren't too worried

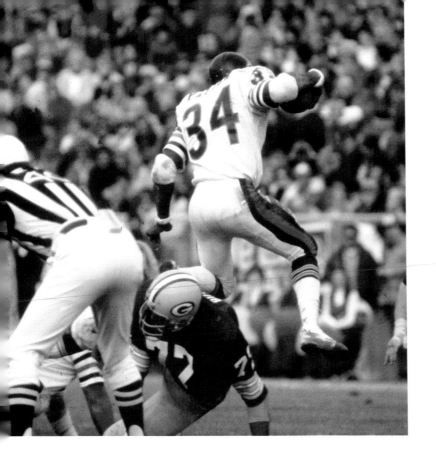

heading out for the kickoff. The Bears had not had the greatest seasons over the past couple of years. They certainly hadn't had any success at Lambeau Field. It seemed like this game would be no different.

But the way it all played out felt almost like divine intervention. We were up 10-7 at halftime, but they shut us down in the third and fourth quarters, and with three minutes to go on the clock they'd pulled ahead 14-13. We drove down and brought the ball to the ten-yard line with seven seconds left. It was just a twenty-eight-yard field goal attempt. It was nothing! It was a shoo-in for us. But they blocked it. Bryan Robinson leapt up—I don't know how he jumped that high—and he got a hand on it. The game was over.

That victory broke a ten-game losing streak for Chicago against Green Bay. Every single player on the field that day felt like Walter was out there, and there's not a doubt in my mind that he had a hand in the Bears' winning that game. It was disheartening for us, of course. I can't say I was happy to take the loss. But I am glad that Walter got one more win to take with him.

There's no doubt that Walter Payton will be remembered as one of the great players of all time. But I think he'll be remembered as much just for being a good guy and an honorable and charitable person. Growing up, and even in my early professional days, I can't say that I was very aware of Walter's foundation work. I think I speak for most guys who are fortunate enough to play professional football when I say that when you're young, your priorities are still on the

field. You don't think about the other stuff as much. But as I've gotten older I've realized how important that kind of charity is, given the position we're in to do things for kids who need help and look up to us. And Walter is a legend in the league just in terms of being a good guy who was very decent and caring and giving of his time. So we all admire him in that way as well.

Walter's mark on the NFL and football is just as great today as it was the day he retired. Right now there's a whole new generation of players coming up through the high schools and colleges down in Mississippi, like I did, and Walter Payton means as much to them as he does to me. He was just a phenomenal player and a phenomenal person who overcame the odds to succeed. He always represented the very best, as a player and as a person. And that's why his legacy lives on today.

The Brothers Payton

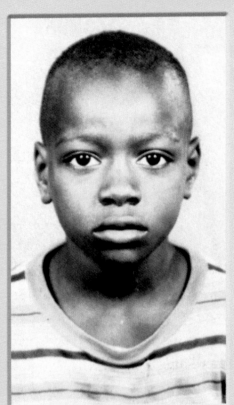

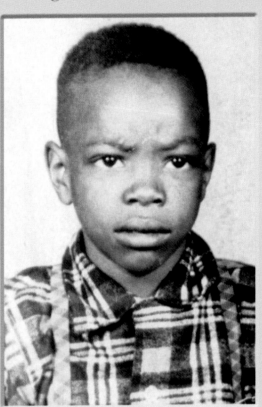

Walter

Eddie

CHAPTER 01 | The Troublemaker

by Connie Payton

Walter always loved a challenge.

Before he tied his first pair of cleats or even held a football, he loved putting his body to the test. Apparently, Walter found an old pair of army boots at the town dump, and he would run all over town in them. His favorite place to run was along the bank of the Pearl River. The muddy, slippery terrain made the outing all the more fun. "You really have to work pretty hard to get going," he once said.

Walter's childhood adventures took him all kinds of places. He used to run wild with Eddie, his older brother, and friends, breaking into abandoned trucks and river barges and jumping onto moving trains. Eddie would chase Walter all over Columbia, Mississippi. They loved to explore the areas around the factory where their parents worked—the woods, the other factories and the pickle plant. "Perfect places for getting into trouble," Walter said.

Walter was always smaller than other kids his age, but he sure did have a stand-out personality. He loved playing pranks. Walter once claimed that he "invented trouble." And he did, especially the time he locked his friend Damon Earl inside a pickle car of a train.

But Walter had such a big imagination that he didn't need to have friends around to have fun. He used to go out into the woods and pretend to be his favorite heroes. He could surround himself in a fantasy world—imagining he was in full costume, riding pretend horses, capturing a pretend enemy. It's possible people passing by on Old Miss Route 35 could have seen him through the brush, prancing around like he was a swashbuckler.

Walter looked back fondly on his childhood games. "When they weren't available or were doing something else, I ran and jumped and played in the woods, pretending I was Robin Hood or some other hero I had seen on television," he recalled. "I might be Sir Lancelot or Zorro. It never occurred to me that these heroes were white. I didn't care. To me, they were good guys instead of bad. They were brave and strong. That's what I wanted to be. A good guy."

Walter's color-blind attitude always helped him to succeed. Also, role-playing helped him to always understand his opponents, which would later come in handy on the football field.

When he was playing out these imaginative adventures, he had to pretend to be both the good guy and the bad guy. So, during these games, Walter learned to understand his opponents' strategies and their reactions. Walter claimed that these lessons were key to his success as an athlete. "And that's why my style is different from other athletes, because it didn't come from athletics," Walter explained. "It came from playing a childhood game. That is something that a coach did not instill in me."

It's funny to think about Walter in his childhood fantasy world, when everywhere around him the country was changing. Some of the most violent events of the civil rights movement took place less than a hundred miles away from Columbia. In 1963, Medgar Evers was shot in front of his home. He bled to death on his concrete porch as his family watched in horror. And they weren't the only ones watching. Anyone could have tuned in to the nightly news to see his body being lifted into an ambulance.

And things only got worse. Members of the Ku Klux Klan executed three young men, white and black, when they traveled to the South to participate in the 1964 Mississippi Freedom Summer. Four little black girls died when racists bombed their church during a Sunday service. And it seemed like time stopped when the assassinations of Martin Luther King and Bobby Kennedy occurred.

All this happening, and there was Walter off playing pranks and pretending to be Zorro.

But it took a long time for change to come to Columbia, Mississippi. It was a stubborn town and held to the traditions of the rural South. Even though the Supreme Court desegregated America's schools in 1954, the year of Walter's birth, Columbia High School shut out the black kids from John J. Jefferson High School until Walter's senior year. The schools were only a mile apart, but that mile made a world of difference.

Columbia was a small town that kept a slow-paced schedule. The noon whistle meant lunch. Lifelong neighbors saw one another nearly every day, and time just seemed to run more slowly there.

By the end of the sixties, Alabama desegregated its schools, and the rest of the South began to follow. The law was the law, and eventually, Columbia took notice. In 1970, they brought the Jefferson kids in from down the road.

Walter was starting to play ball at an exciting time. His performance on the field, and the victories that he helped secure for Columbia, became a way to unite the town and make everyone feel they were on the same team. He helped demonstrate just how well black and white kids could work together.

Though Walter became a champion Wildcat, he had only been playing football since his sophomore year. He had stayed away from the football field because Eddie had been the star of the Jefferson Green Wave. Also, Walter was preoccupied by his other extracurricular activities. He was student-body president at Jefferson. He was also the snare drummer for the school band, and boy, did he love that.

Apparently, throughout his freshman year, Charles Boston, who coached all Jefferson sports, was putting pressure on Walter to join the football team. But Walter wouldn't give in. Eventually, though, I think he sensed the time was right. "Once my brother graduated and some of those great players were gone, I thought I might enjoy football," he said.

Boston remembers having his eye on the Payton brothers for some time. He used to pass their house on Hendricks Street on his way to and from school, and he would watch Eddie and Walter run and play around the yard. He also caught Walter in a few pick-up football games on the playground. And like all great coaches, he had a sixth sense about Walter's bob-and-weave style and Eddie's quicks and intelligence on Columbia's sandlots. But once he landed Eddie on the team, Boston couldn't convince their mother Alyne Payton, or Walter, for that matter, to let her youngest join his brother on the field. I suspect Alyne thought it best for Walter to be Walter, to play his snare drum and goof around a little before he made such a major commitment.

With Eddie's scholarship to Jackson State secured, finally, in 1968, Boston convinced Alyne and Walter that the time to focus on his future had arrived. Walter agreed on one condition: that he could play Jefferson ball without giving up his position with the school band. Walter was still hesitant, like all little brothers facing the burden of filling an older brother's larger shoes, but he took a deep breath and stepped out onto the field for the first time. It did not come easily.

W
i
l
d
c
a
t
s

'70

The Columbia High student body really had something to cheer for this season. The Cats had a successful year, winning 8 and losing only 2. The support was enthusiastic, and all of C.H.S. pulled for the mighty cats. We really think all the Wildcat coaches and players are the best, and we know next year they can reach the number 1 spot in the South Little Dixie Conference.

C
o
a
c
h
e
s

BOSTON
end coach

DAVIS
head coach

BARNES
back coach

PATRICK
line coach

40

He was just terrified of the game during his first few practices. He once wrote, "I had never worn the pads and all that stuff, and I didn't know the first thing about real fundamentals." But even worse, his first touchdown in his first practice came by running into the wrong end zone. The way he told the story, he was petrified by the thought of being tackled by his larger teammates, so he just ran to the closest end zone. He nearly did the same thing during the second play, but froze in embarrassment a few yards short of the Jefferson High School Hall of Shame. Eventually, he got the hang of it, and with the paternal Boston guiding his development as well as the other talents on the team, the Jefferson Green Wave became a tightly bound team.

I think in those last years of segregation, Boston felt some particular internal pressure to make Jefferson not just as good as other teams in the area, but the best. And he did. Just before Columbia and Jefferson became a single team, Boston had led the Green Waves to seven straight victories.

In 1970, almost like something out of the movie script *Remember the Titans*, Boston traveled with his players to become a Columbia Wildcat. He became the assistant coach, the second in command to Columbia's white coach, Tommy Davis.

Walter didn't dwell on the transition, nor did many other members of the Green Wave. And besides, most Columbia folks—black and white—shrugged off the racial politics of the era as media hype. He even said to a journalist who was covering that first week of integration in Columbia, "…If you would just leave us alone, we will get along just fine."

Walter had reason to believe that everyone would get along just fine. There were signs of respect between the two communities from the start. The schools had decided that he could go on as student-body president after desegregation. He shared the title with the Columbia High president. And it soon became clear that Walter would become a real leader on the playing field.

The biggest problem with desegregation for Walter and his teammates, as one would expect with competitive young men, was not the mixing of black and white but the mixing of rival football squads. The teams from Jefferson and Columbia had been playing against each other for years, and their rivalry was akin to Hatfields against McCoys. So things were very tense at the beginning.

One of the best Columbia players, Ricky Joe Graves, spoke about the beginning of the season with the new combined team. "I'll never forget that first day of spring practice," he says. "All the blacks were on one end of the field, and all the whites were on the other side of the field. Of course, we had heard that Walter was supposed to be pretty good. We were bragging, 'Yeah, I'm gonna put him on the ground, blah, blah, blah.'"

As Columbia's best hitter, Graves took it upon himself to make a statement for the Wildcats. He would plant the young Green Wave in the ground, and depending upon how well the running back took his medicine, he might help Walter back up. That way, he'd firmly establish the pecking order of the team, and they might be able to put all of the racial garbage behind them. And quick.

"So they ran this one particular play, and I knew that Walter was going to get the football, and I knew where he was going to be. All I had to do was get to a point. When the ball was snapped, I just took off and was going to meet him there. Well, I did meet him there, and, boy, I laid into him. I thought, man, I got this sucker. And I just laid everything into him. I had him almost on the ground, almost horizontal. I wrapped up on him and everything. The next thing I felt was his knees hitting me right under the chin, and he was running again, and I'm sprawled out on the ground after being dodoed. And he was gone for a touchdown. Walter just ran over me. It was just unreal, the balance that he had."

I think those boys must have realized that times were changing for

WALTER PAYTON
Fullback

Columbia. But it never happened through demonstrations or violence—it really happened right out there with Walter, on the football field. All around the country whites were upset about change and desegregation, but Walter showed the town of Columbia that this change was a good thing. He was going to lead all of them to the championship, and in the process, he united the town by giving them something to root for and be proud of.

Those Jefferson players brought a championship record to the Wildcats, between the seven straight victories and Walter's scoring record from directly before desegregation. So I think even from the beginning the Wildcats knew it was a good thing.

Even Coach Boston saw the changes play out on the field. "I was even happy when they stopped playing 'Dixie' at the Columbia High football games," he recalls. "I think people began to see the kids as Wildcats instead of a white boy or a black boy or whatever. I think that really helped integration here at Columbia. I think it was a big reason there was no trouble here."

Walter never really thought about the race issue, even when all this was going on around him. He always said that he had no grudges against the Columbia kids, because it wasn't their fault that all this was happening. But he was competitive with them. He said the only thing dividing the students was the fact that those Jefferson kids wanted to do better than the Columbia kids—in the band, on the field, in everything.

And ultimately, all that mattered for Walter when he was on the field was his love for the game.

He played his heart out during that first season as a Wildcat. Apparently, during their first game of that '70 season, no one could keep up with him as he dodged and darted around players. They were playing against Prentiss High. And there were twenty-five hundred fans in the stands to watch him lead the Wildcats to a win. His Columbia teammates still talk about it. "We were trailing in the first half 6-0 when Walter got the ball in just a little, simple dive play, and he went for ninety-five," says Columbia player Forest Dantin. "Just as he cleared around the thirty-yard line, he just kind of coasted. Then somebody on the other team kind of showed up in the background, and he looked behind him and saw him. It was just like he hit another gear. He was gone. He was in the end zone."

You know, even back then Walter was showing the way he would play until his last days on Soldier Field. He had this unreal speed, graceful agility and a forceful attack that, together, made him unstoppable. And back then, he was only 165 pounds. And still, no one could stop him.

By the time Walter finished high school as a Wildcat, he had come a long way. People don't realize that he had some upsets at the beginning of his career on the field.

"I'd skip through the line, turning and digging and trying to accelerate," Walter wrote. "But when somebody cut off my route, I lowered both head and shoulder and drove into him. More and more often, the second time a guy came at me, he remembered that first shot he'd taken from me." He had learned just how he wanted to play on the field.

And off the field, Walter had also learned some serious lessons about will and dedication. His parents, Alyne and Peter Payton, worked double shifts at Columbia's hometown manufacturing plant to support Walter, Eddie and Pamela. Peter Payton—a stoic, hardworking and purposeful man—led by example, not by speechifying. His life's work taught his sons and his daughter to live their lives according to his favorite motto:

If you start something, you shouldn't quit.
If you're going to play, you might as well play to be your best.

WALTER PAYTON

Knowledge comes, but wisdom lingers.

CHAPTER

 02 | The Dancing Tiger

by Connie Payton

In the spring of his senior year, when all the college recruiters were calling, Walter pretty much sat back and waited for the offers to start rolling in. He was, after all, clearly the best high-school football player in the state of Mississippi and, quite possibly, in the entire South. But in 1971, even elite black athletes were in no way guaranteed acceptance into major Division I programs. Alabama's legendary Paul "Bear" Bryant, knowing full well that open recruiting of talented black athletes could win him national championships, said at the time, "I won't be the first to let in black players… but I won't be the last."

Back in Columbia, as worse players than Walter were receiving scholarships and signing letters of intent, Coach Boston was shaking his head in dismay. Walter's teammate Steve Stewart, a white player and a fine wide receiver in his own right, signed with the University of Mississippi while Walter barely got a sniff, even though the school was only thirty miles east of Columbia. "It was the times," Coach Boston shrugs.

But Coach Boston made sure that his alma mater, Alcorn State, courted Walter, as did "Payton University North," Jackson State. But the only major Division I school that had a serious interest in Walter was Kansas.

Gale Sayers

The University of Kansas already had some success by taking a chance on a small-town black kid back in 1960. The quiet young man from Omaha, Nebraska, arrived at Kansas a little too small to be taken seriously, but ended up as a two-time all-American dubbed the "Kansas Comet." He went on to star in the National Football League and was winding down a career with the Chicago Bears. A few years later, he would enter the NFL Hall of Fame and the public's eternal consciousness as the author of *I Am Third*. His autobiography would be adapted for the screen as *Brian's Song*. The Kansas Jayhawks correctly suspected that the young Walter Payton could be their next Gale Sayers.

The fact that Eddie was already playing at Jackson State should have made Walter's choice an obvious and fairly easy one. But this was Walter, after all. His decision-making process was starting to resemble his on-field running style: as much sideline to sideline and reversal of field as going straight ahead.

Kansas was pushing hard and was an intriguing destination. For a small town boy like Walter, the University of Kansas offered an opportunity to sample a way of life very different from his upbringing. Also, if he went to Kansas, Walter would get out from under the shadow of Eddie, to whom he was so often compared. But he also knew that he'd be stepping into another equally formidable shadow: Sayers's.

*A dapper coach Hill with his prize player,
an equally dapper Walter Payton*

Jackson State had its own allure: familiarity, comfort and the chance to play *alongside* his brother, now that they could be teammates. And then there was the Jackson Tigers' head coach, Bob Hill, a man who would make a huge impression on Walter and would profoundly influence our lives. Coach Hill was not only a great football coach, he turned out to be a pretty decent matchmaker as well—it was at Bob Hill's urging that I would be fixed up on a blind date with his young star running back. But I'm getting ahead of myself. That would come later.

Coach Hill, tough, intimidating and no-nonsense, commanded respect. He expected all of his players to bleed for him on the field while notching victories *and* to attend all of their classes and get their degrees. After visiting the campus and watching the Tigers suffer through Coach Hill's Marine-style training in the sweltering heat of a typical Mississippi summer day, Walter was sold. "I think I want to go here," he told Eddie.

But that was far from a promise or binding obligation, and Kansas, still in the hunt, was pushing hard. Walter, unprepared for the intense pressure coming at him, was still weighing his options, even when Coach Hill was forcing the issue. Walter explained, "Coach Hill was anxious to get me to sign a letter committing myself exclusively to Jackson State…so when Coach Hill finally said he wanted my brother and me to go with him to Columbia to get my letter of agreement signed, I felt torn. We drove down there one afternoon, and while Eddie and Coach Hill were talking with my parents, I snuck out. I took my dad's car, picked up my neighbor John Gralin and headed back to Jackson State. All I knew was that I was tired of trying to make my own decisions. Inside, I wanted someone to advise me, but on the surface I was just running."

After goofing around with Gralin in Jackson and driving back home, Walter discovered that Coach Hill and Eddie were still in his family's house on Hendrick Street talking with his parents. So he drove away again, this time just riding around town rather than having to step back into the house to tell them he had just driven to Jackson and back. Walter only returned once Coach Hill had left and taken Eddie back up to school that night.

So after an extremely long day of driving hundreds of miles and getting nowhere, Walter finally went back to the house where his mother was waiting. Walter's indecisive nature was apparently not hereditary. His mom informed him, "If you can't make up your mind where you want to go to school, I'll make it up for you. You're going to Jackson State." Walter recollected, "Strangely, my fear and confusion lifted. I knew that others couldn't make decisions for me all my life, but this school business had swept down upon me too quickly. I was glad to have it finally settled."

Once Walter donned the #34 jersey—big brother Eddie remained #22— the Tigers' backfield was quickly labeled "Payton's Place." Jackie Slater, a college teammate who—like many JSU alums—would go on to the NFL and a remarkable seventeen-year Hall of Fame career remembers, "Many of us could not understand how it could even be fathomed that Walter could be better than Eddie, because Eddie was just a fantastic little tough guy. But then we saw it."

Jackson State teammate Rodney Phillips recalls, "The first time he really impressed me was his freshman year. I was sitting out as a 'redshirt' that year, and I was watching practice. They put Walter out on the practice field with the older guys, and they gave him the ball, and he just started running over people. Those he didn't run over he ran around, and then nobody could catch him. Everybody else had been working out and practicing and was older, and he came out there the first day and blew them all away. And you have to remember how good the other players were. There were probably a couple dozen future pros on that field, a lot of future first-round NFL picks, NFL starters. So this was no simple thing."

The talent pool in black colleges does not escape the microscope of the National Football League. It's no secret among NFL scouts that the first stops for any recruiter worth his salt are schools like Alcorn State, Mississippi Valley State, Grambling and Jackson State for prime draft material. The alumni of these schools include Steve McNair, Jerry Rice and Doug Williams.

Walter's adjustment to college life was made easier because he was rooming not only with Eddie, but also with Edward "Sugarman" Moses (also from home). Life under Coach Hill was regimented and disciplined, with long and exhausting days. According to Walter, "At night, we couldn't wait to go to the room and go to sleep. And believe me, we were afraid to get in trouble. He probably would have taken you out and spanked your butt just like a parent would do."

On the field, Walter realized that Coach Hill's respect could not be won by dazzling him with running ability alone. While Walter's moves were impressive, it was really Walter's blocking, kicking (he'd become JSU's placekicker as well as its star running back) and all-out hustle that enamored him to Hill. The harder the coach pushed his players past what they thought they could endure, the more obvious it became that Walter simply refused to be outworked. The pairing of Coach Hill and Walter was a match made

in heaven: a demanding coach and a tireless star, both searching to be their best, period, not just better than anyone else.

Walter once told a reporter about a game in his first year in which Kentucky State was leading the Tigers 14-0 going into halftime: "As we sat there drinking our Cokes and trying to catch a second wind, he stormed in, holding his clipboard with both hands. He strode over to fullback Ricky Young and whopped him on the helmet with his clipboard. 'You call that running the ball? And Payton, you're not running, you're playin' hopscotch out there!' WHOP! He banged me on the helmet." Then Hill shoved his Tigers back onto the field. Kentucky never scored another point. Jackson State won the game 28-14.

But even the tough drill instructor of a coach had a softer side. Walter's amazing ability was not limited to the football field, so it came as no surprise when he appeared with a dance partner in an early hip-hop-style routine on television's *Soul Train*. In fact, the very first time I ever saw Walter Payton, I had no idea who he was other than a really good dancer I was watching on television as a high-school senior back home in New Orleans.

Now, truth be told, when I was a senior in high school my Aunt Betty was dating Coach Hill. Coach Hill would often talk about Walter and how he thought we might hit it off. Of course, Coach also had football on his mind and probably thought it a good idea to trim Walter's ever-growing female fan base so that he could channel Walter's energy even deeper into football. For whatever reason, he just thought that I would be a nice, sensible girlfriend for Walter. He gave Walter my home number, and one day when I answered the phone, I was very surprised to hear Walter's distinctive, high-pitched voice on the other end. Walter was calling from a counselor's office at Jackson State. And we talked for hours.

Not long after that, I flew up to Jackson for a visit. Coach Hill picked me

up at the airport and drove us back to his house. I remember he had a long row of pictures of Jackson State players hanging on a wall in the living room. He pointed to them and asked, "Which of those young men do you think is him?" I had no idea. So I went down the line looking at the pictures, saying to myself, "Oh, man, please don't let it be this one," or "He's sort of nice looking." And of course I picked the wrong picture! Walter's picture was one of the ones I'd passed by. But then I took a second look, and I remember saying to Coach Hill, "Okay, he's not that bad."

I wouldn't say our date was memorable in the romantic sense; it really was because Walter continued to talk about his ex-girlfriend. And I recall thinking, "I just hope he can get back together with this girl, because it sounds like he really likes her." After our date, we drove back to Coach Hill's house, and I didn't know if I would ever hear from him again.

Some time had passed since our date when Walter called and wanted to come to New Orleans to visit me and to meet my parents. I remember the dinner being what must have been uncomfortable for Walter, because he was so nervous he wouldn't eat. He wouldn't even put food on his plate, which totally annoyed my mother. His insistence on not eating annoyed me later that evening, when Walter complained that he was starving and asked if I would make him something to eat. He asked for a bowl of cereal or anything. Naturally, I was thinking, "What am I getting myself into?"

The next year, I enrolled at Jackson State. I became a member of the school's Jaycettes marching band and danced at halftime for the JSU Tigers.

Walter's game just kept improving. On October 11, 1973, a column appeared in the *Jackson Clarion-Ledger* that advertised what everybody in town already knew to be true: "Walter Payton, Jackson State halfback who the Tigers refer to as their Heisman Trophy candidate, just can't stop dancing, either on or off the field. On the field, the five foot eleven, two hundred pounder danced his way to nearly a thousand yards rushing and receiving last year and scored seventeen points, and he threatens to top those figures as he has over six hundred yards rushing and sixty points in five games this season."

That year when the Heisman was awarded, Jackson held its breath, but then the 1973 award went to running back…John Cappelletti of Penn State, the white-shirted, black-shoed East Coast powerhouse. Then the trophy went to another East Coast titan, Ohio State's running back Archie Griffin, not once but for *two* years in a row. After that, Walter was understandably deflated. While both solid players, neither Cappelletti nor Griffin was in Walter's league. In fact, they would both go on to play only briefly in the NFL. The players came from two of the highest-profile, big-time programs in the country, and the schools' well-oiled publicity machinery surely advanced the causes of their respective athletes in ways that a Jackson State could never hope to compete against.

Outwardly, Walter tried to make it seem like he wasn't angry about it. Still, a teammate at the time tells of watching an Ohio State game on TV

with him once in a dorm room: "All of a sudden Walter sat up on the edge of the bed, and you could tell he was upset. I said, 'Man, what's the matter with you?' He said some expletives and then said, 'Archie Griffin can't carry my jock.'" And then when reporters asked him about the issue, his feelings spilled out. There was an article, buried inside the January 14, 1975, issue of the *Atlanta Constitution*, where Walter, goaded by a reporter to compare himself to Griffin and Anthony Davis, another Heisman finalist, said curtly, "No comparison. I'm better than they are, and I know it."

But even with this knowledge, and despite being a finalist (again!) in his senior year, Walter never did win the Heisman. That, too, was part and parcel of being a gifted black athlete attending a small school in Mississippi in the mid-seventies. So, as Walter was preparing to hang up his Tigers jersey, he had no inkling that a much bigger challenge awaited him just beyond graduation.

In 1975, Chicago Bears director of pro scouting Bill Tobin attended an all-star game that included a number of potential NFL draft picks. After watching the players on the field for a while, Tobin remembers hearing another scout next to him pointing out a slim, black kid not even on the field. "That's that running back at Jackson State that everyone's talking about," Tobin remembers the man saying. So Tobin took another look. And he started to discover what Boston and Hill already knew: this kid would outrun and outplay anyone, if only given the shot.

No one wanted that shot more than Walter. I remember the day as if it were yesterday. We were all together, because Jackson State had about six or seven guys who were believed to be going pretty high in the draft. There had also been talk that Walter would be going in the first round. This rumor proved to be true, when the Chicago Bears used their first round pick on January 28, 1975—fourth overall behind Steve Bartkoswki (Atlanta Falcons),

Randy White (Dallas Cowboys) and Ken Huff (Baltimore Colts)—to select Walter as the first running back chosen in the draft. With the success of the NFL draft under their belts, Walter and his JSU teammates hit the pavement on rented motorcycles for a long day of joyrides. Robert Brazile, Walter's Jackson State linebacker teammate, was chosen just two slots later as the first-round pick (number six overall) of the Houston Oilers.

With Walter growing up in the South, we were wondering how he would "bear" the weather. He did just fine! All kidding aside, his move to

Walter was an academic standout at Jackson State University. Completing his undergraduate work early, he graduated while working on a Masters degree.

Chicago proved to be an adjustment all the way around. And it was all good. From the beginning, Walter thrived on wanting to do well for his newfound family, the Chicago Bears. For the Bears management, the dream was that Walter would prove to be the lynchpin for a brand new Chicago Bear era. And Walter would move mountains to make their dreams come true.

Though the Chicago Bears briefly showed promise with the arrival of Gale Sayers and Dick Butkus in 1965, the seventies had proven to be seriously hard times. But Papa George Halas, who proved to be a caring mentor, would no longer tolerate abysmal play, and he personally reached out to Walter to instill the essential character of BEARNESS in the young man. Little did Halas know that his pupil was well versed in the art of delayed gratification and hard work.

On that cold January day, I don't know if any one person realized the magic that would be made between Walter and the city of Chicago.

CHAPTER 03 | Stinging Defeats

Zero yards.

After the first pro game of his career, all Walter Payton had to show for himself was eight carries for zero yards. In the aftermath of the Bears' humiliating 35-7 opening-day loss to the Baltimore Colts, Payton walked off the field with "zero yards" tattooed on his brain.

For the long-suffering Chicago fans filing to the exits, 1975 was already shaping up to be yet another year of cursed hopes and blown opportunities. In spite of their recent roster reshuffling, new training facility and the addition of a lynchpin running back (how many times had fans heard that before?), the brand-new Bears looked a heckuva lot like the same old seventies sad sacks.

Like every other Bears fan, the *Chicago Tribune*'s Don Pierson had winced through the abysmal performance of head coach Abe Gibron's starting lineup for years. "Gibron's teams were really awful," Pierson remembers. "They were tough teams and played hard—Dick Butkus was on those teams—but they were terrible and didn't really have much of a chance."

In 1974, after TV cameras caught Gibron clowning and singing during yet another Bears loss, the NFL's most loyal fans demanded his head. And with the Bears finishing the '74 season with a 4-10 record—dead last for the third season in a row—the Bears' front office prepared the platter. General manager Jim Finks axed Gibron, and, for the first time in their history, the Bears hired a head coach from outside the insular Bear organization. But they found a Bear kind of coach in Jack Pardee.

A Texas A&M Aggie all-American and a famed member of Coach Paul "Bear" Bryant's "Junction Boys," Pardee took his college bona fides and built on them in the NFL as a player. A fourteenth overall pick in the 1957 NFL draft, Pardee was a longtime veteran linebacker for the Rams and then the Redskins, with two All-Pro seasons. After an amazing one-year record as head coach of the upstart Florida Blazers of the World Football League (he led them to the WFL championship game and a record of 14-6), Pardee grabbed the opportunity to lead the storied Chicago Bear franchise.

Pardee's arrival at Bears training camp was as keenly anticipated as any player's. Any player except Walter Payton, that is.

The Bears came to the 1975 NFL draft to shop, and Jackson State's star rusher, Walter Payton, was at the top of their list. But Chicago's brain trust had to wait its turn behind three teams just as desperate for new blood as the Bears. Front-office rumors that the Cowboys were interested in Payton were circulating. But Jim Finks and company breathed a sigh of relief when Dallas, thinking they'd get more years out of a defensive tackle than a running back, chose University of Maryland's Randy White over Payton. No one could know that White and Payton would both retire thirteen years later with tickets thoroughly punched for entrance into the Hall of Fame.

Finks personally called Payton to welcome him to the Bears and let him know that he was the team's first choice. For NFL cellar teams like the 1970s Bears, draft day becomes the fan base's own private form of Super Bowl. With its reverse order selection system (worst teams first, best teams last), the draft itself is an ingenious design. The system gives the lowliest spirit-sapped football fan an annual renewal of hope. For one draft choice, and the addition of that one prize player to a team, can transform a cellar dweller into a contender. In 1975, hope sprang eternal in the Second City that a man named Payton could turn the Doormats of the Midway back into Monsters.

But as any fan knows, with hope come equal quantities of cynicism. And the early word on the street was that Walter was a little too small, a little too slow and a little too green to be the alchemist that Bears fans were looking for. In fact, with another strong runner—Mike Adamle—already on the roster, his starting position in the backfield was not even locked up. Pierson remembers how a preeminent sports magazine painted Payton as "just another small-black-college running back who liked to play the drums—it was almost a racist comment." So while on one page of the Chicago dailies Payton's draft was hailed as a front-office triumph, on the next it seemed as if the papers were asking, "Walter who?"

Payton's friend and lawyer Bud Holmes had been legal counsel to the New Orleans Saints, but the Michigan Avenue dailies described him as an aw-shucks and duplicitous country lawyer straight out of *Green Acres.* So when a last-minute change in plans forced Payton to change his arrival time in Chicago, the press reported that Bears officials sent to O'Hare to greet Payton were left standing at the gate. The fact that Walter and Holmes had asked for and received a signing bonus bigger than the one Ole Miss star Archie Manning (father of Peyton and Eli Manning) had received from the Saints got around, too.

Loyal and hardworking, Chicagoans expect nothing from new arrivals that they don't demand of themselves. After a decade of wasted talent, and especially since the death of Brian Piccolo, Chicago's football fans were shell-shocked. They needed a reason not to write off their home team as an

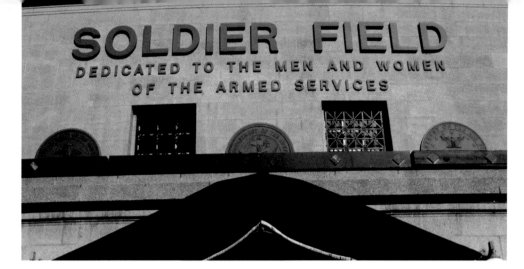

unfortunate fact of Second City life like the arctic blasts from Lake Michigan in winter. Bears fans wanted to believe that their team's first-round draft choice was more than just another off-season front-office gamble. They needed proof.

So in the aftermath of that dismal '75 season opener, Bears fans couldn't be blamed for having some hard questions. Zero yards? We went in two-point favorites and lost by four touchdowns? Zero yards? This is the NCAA's all-time leading rusher? Zero yards? This is what you get from a new roster and a new coach? Zero yards? This is Walter Payton? Meet the new Bears, same as the old Bears.

But what the fans couldn't know was that Payton was asking himself the very same questions. He needed proof, too.

Boss-mayor Richard E. Daley liked to call his town "The City that Works," and no one believed in hard work more than Payton. He was a man who never made excuses and was interested only in results. Payton drove himself further and harder than anyone in the stands could ever have suspected after only seeing his debut against the Colts. He drove himself with a determination and strength that every Bears fan would come to know in time. Echoing a man who worked harder than anyone he would ever know, Walter recalled that first Bears defeat: "I wasn't going to quit. I wasn't going to change the way I did things."

If you start something, you shouldn't quit. If you're going to play, you might as well play to be your best.

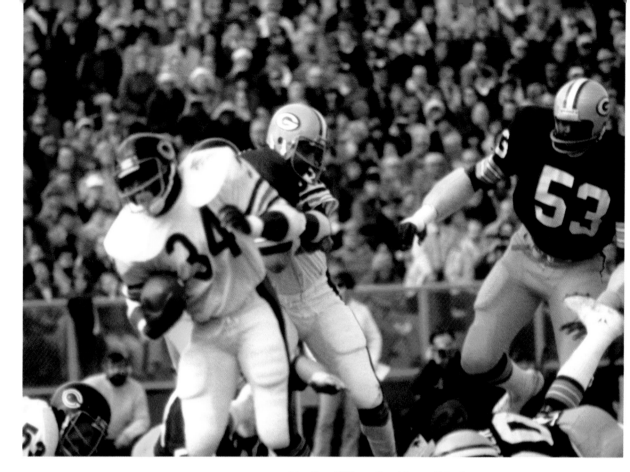

Up the Hill at the Line of Scrimmage

How Payton started things was with a training regimen that would have stopped lesser men cold. During his senior year at Jackson State, he discovered a towering sandbank on the shore of the Pearl River. He'd found the terrain that he knew could take him to a personal best in strength and endurance. Payton paced off a sixty-five yard course and dubbed it simply "the Sand," as if it were a place to bring a cooler of cold drinks, an umbrella and sunscreen.

Because of the loose surface and the steep angle, five dozen yards plus five up the Sand was the same as a football field and a half of turf. He'd lower his center of gravity, cut left, cut right, bob, twist and drive up the hill to simulate runs at the line of scrimmage, where little quarter was given.

On his way down, he accelerated when the natural impulse was to tiptoe, sliced left, sliced right, shifted his momentum and stiff-armed imaginary tacklers to simulate the chase of an open-field dash. And he

did it in the midday, 106-degree Mississippi heat. To gain physical advantage over circumstances he couldn't otherwise change—his two-hundred-pound body versus three-hundred-pound defensive linemen at the line and his average running back speed against lightning-quick defensive backs in the open field—he'd work like his father worked before him. With purpose.

The Sand soon forged an inimitable running style that ensured a place at the NFL table. It was impossible to do controlled cuts in sand without solidly planting each step before taking the next. As Payton pounded up and down the dunes, he swung his legs from the hips instead of bending his knees. He clubbed his feet into shifting sand. He wasn't just running, he was digging in and taking off, stride by stride. On the Sand, the "dancing moves" he'd demonstrated at Columbia Wildcats games gained stability and pile-driver intensity.

Down the Hill in the Open Field

But the Sand proved far more potent as a training tool—it gave Walter the desire and ultimately the ability to carve into his own private pain threshold. What separates professional athletes from legendary athletes is not the dominance of their physical attributes; rather, it is the size of their hearts and minds that takes them to Olympian heights. By whittling away his core pain intolerance, Walter found his secret superhero weapon, far stronger than Spiderman's web and more lethal than Zorro's sword. While others' pain weakened them, Walter used his pain to grow stronger.

The Sand begat the Levee, and the Levee begat the Stairs.

Carving deeper and deeper into himself, Walter ran ruts in "the Levee," a short, forty-five-degree rise on the river levee near Jackson State, and tore up his quads on the punishing, nearly vertical steps of the Jackson State stadium. His internal steeling of himself became a physical mantra.

Ten times up and down the Sand, twenty times up and down the Levee, and an hour straight in brutal Mississippi heat on the stadium steps.

And he did it alone.

But every now and then a tough and competitive Jackson State Tiger would join him with every intention of completing Walter's circuit. Walter would smile and laugh his laugh as he watched each of them first lose his wind, then his lunch and then his will. Not one took more out of the Sand than it took out of him. Walter would pat them on the back, leave them with one last giggle and jog along to the Levee.

This was the way Payton approached preseason training—flat out, no compromise, pushing his natural ability beyond its already remarkable threshold and into a realm not seen since. Payton maintained this grueling regimen his entire career. First it was on the hills and steps of Columbia when he returned home after his rookie season as a Bear, and then on a

made-to-order, unrelentingly punishing incline he discovered near his new home in Chicago's Arlington Heights in the late seventies. And through every workout, he carried that first-game defeat up the hill with him:

"When I worked that hill, training and killing myself over the years, I often began by saying, 'Zero yards!' That was to remind me of that game. I remembered how I felt that first day, and really the entire season, and tried to use that in my leadership later in my playing career. People often asked how I never got discouraged during some of the lean years and how I continued to be a professional. Well, that's why."

Payton's perception of his own performance was, by his own definition, unforgiving, but his new teammates could see Payton's eagerness and commitment during training camp. And even after the Colt drubbing, they saw a crystal ball of possibilities. "Zero yards, but it was like I'd just watched someone gain 150," Bears teammate and rival starter Mike Adamle recalls. "He made a couple of moves in the backfield after he was stopped for losses, just to get back to the line of scrimmage, and I said, 'This guy's great.' And he got zero yards."

Driving himself came naturally to Payton. Settling in did not. It hadn't helped that he'd missed the first two weeks of training camp in order to work out for the college all-star game in August of '75. It also hadn't helped that he'd injured his elbow while training for the All-Stars and then kept reinjuring it once he reported to the Bears. His elbow had repeatedly sidelined him during the preseason. He watched his team march down the road to opening day from the bench.

Payton's first start was the next-to-last game of the Bears' preseason and took place in the oppressive late-summer heat of Miami's Orange Bowl. Concerned for his new running back's elbow, Jack Pardee had intended to keep Payton in the game for only the first half. But after

gaining sixty yards on twelve carries during the first two quarters, Payton stayed in for the third and finished strong with the highest single game total of the preseason. With his elbow injury finally behind him, Payton assumed his regular season debut would be just as spectacular. But the Colts proved otherwise.

The following week, the Bears faced the Philadelphia Eagles with open eyes and renewed determination. When the dust settled after a nail-biting fourth quarter, the Bears had stolen a 15-13 win on a field goal with just eight seconds left on the clock. And Payton played the kind of smart and gutsy game that would become his professional signature. Despite two fifteen-yard penalties, he straight-armed his way through twenty-one carries and caught six of quarterback Gary Huff's passes for a combined total of 131 yards.

The victory was sweet, but not sweet enough to take the bitter taste off the five straight losses that followed. Payton may have held his own against the Vikings' dreaded "Purple People Eater" front four, but his team was clobbered 28-3 by Fran Tarkenton's offense. They fared little better against Detroit, which repeated the Colts' pounding and shut down Payton's ten carrying attempts, pummeling the Bears into the snowy Detroit turf 27-7. Chicago then fell to Pittsburgh before getting manhandled by Tarkenton's Vikings a second time.

Nothing was coming easy. Even when Payton scored his first NFL touchdown against the Dolphins, it was only the fifth Bears TD of the season, and they couldn't win that game either. By mid-season, the Bears had posted their worst record since the halfway mark of 1969's ghastly 1-13 yearlong freefall. Zero yards was a curse they couldn't shake. It may not have felt like it at the time, but their mutual suffering was forcing the team together. They may have avoided the faces of some fans and certain reporters, but they were honest with each other.

Payton stayed as close to his team off the field as on. "During even the toughest years, when we couldn't buy a win, he'd always make everyone laugh," remembers Roland Harper, Payton's best friend on the team. His class-clown days at Columbia High and at Jackson were far from over. "He was famous for his fireworks. He loved the M-80s because they were the loudest," Harper says. "One time he set one off in the lobby of our training camp in the middle of the night. It was during 'two-a-days,' so everyone was exhausted. The police and fire departments came. The police knew Payton had done it, so they went to his room. By the time they got there, he had snuck out a window and had set the sirens on their cars off."

The Bears needed a sense of humor. The second half of Payton's rookie season was nearly as infuriating as the first. But even as the Bears posted four more losses out of their final seven, Payton was learning. Whether it was dragging Green Bay's Johnny Gray into the end zone for a touchdown, helping Chicago dash Detroit's wild-card playoff hopes or getting skinned alive by the Rams, Payton was learning the ins and outs and the ups and downs of NFL team play. More importantly, he was learning that, despite his doubts, he had the stuff it took to play the game at the highest level. A losing season offered no shortcuts. Adversity hardened him. It focused his skills. Relentless defeat was a trial by a fire far hotter than the Mississippi sun that beat down on the Sand.

Payton was learning to work with his blockers—to anticipate the holes they would tear open for him in an opposing team's defense. He was learning to smell the oncoming blitz in the air like a gathering thundershower. In a 31-3 shelling in San Francisco, he learned about the irresistible onslaught of a great passing game. In the snows of Green Bay, he learned how to keep fighting when it seemed like his very soul was frozen inside himself. He was finding his abilities, pushing his envelope, testing himself and his opponents. He was learning how to play *his* game at a professional level.

At five foot ten and two hundred pounds, "Sweetness" was shorter and lighter than many other players. "I was quick, but not fast," Payton remembered. Against an avalanche of bigger and faster players, he had to improvise, to deflect, to unite his mind and his body into a single potent combination of reflex and intelligence. He had to make his adversaries do all the guessing. He did, and it worked. "I'd stutter-step. Opponents didn't know what you were going to do. They didn't know if you were going to go straight, if you were going to come at them or if you were going to stop. When you do that he has to think, and then it gives you that edge and you can go right by him. I had to do all sorts of tricks like that."

But Payton learned the hardest lesson of that hardest of all seasons on the bench. Expecting to suit up against the Steelers, Payton instead sat the game out because of a bruised ankle. He was shocked at the coaching staff's decision. "I was like, 'excuse me, an ankle?'" he remembered. He'd been "staying physical," as Pardee liked to urge his players to do, for most of an epically grueling season. Miss a game for a sore ankle? It seemed ridiculous—he'd played through much worse.

At Jackson, he'd have simply ignored it. "I got it taped three times. I taped the skin without any prewrap because they said it would hold better. Then I put on my sock and taped it again. Finally I put on my shoe, and they wrapped it up. I gained one hundred something yards and scored a couple of touchdowns that day. So I figured if I could do it in Jackson, I could do it in Chicago," he recalled. His full-contact, stutter-step style had netted him bruised knees, elbows, shoulders—just about every ache and pain imaginable.

"When you have pain, what you do is you focus on non-pain," he once said. "You focus your mind on soothing. You focus your mind on creating a healing form. I've had injuries that for some people would have taken them three and four weeks to heal from, but with me it would only take three and four days. The reason I healed quickly is that I didn't dwell on the pain." But Pardee was adamant. It was his decision to make, and he made it. Payton sat out the game. It would be the only game he missed for the rest of his thirteen-year career. "What I learned that day," Payton admitted, "was that I didn't get to make that call." By benching Payton, Pardee was treating him as an invaluable asset: an unsung hero of this season and the secret weapon for next season. But he wasn't the only one who saw what number thirty-four had brought to the team.

Payton had been embarrassed by preseason headlines trumpeting him as the new Gale Sayers. But, as Chicago's last game of the 1975 season

approached, the same sentiment began to quietly echo from Chicago's fans themselves. Despite the Bears' dismal performance as a team that year, Payton was beginning to get some recognition. "Chicago fans respected players who worked hard," remembers Payton's brother Eddie. "They can appreciate effort. For so long the Bears were pretty mediocre—what they didn't have was effort. What Payton brought was a period of effort. Even if they didn't win, the effort was there every week."

The Bears' final game of the excruciating 1975 season cemented that respect. This time, Walter Payton was doing the teaching. On December 21 he ran roughshod over the New Orleans Saints on their home turf. As if driven to prove once and for all to his team and its fans that he was more than just another promising rookie prospect, Payton scorched the Superdome like wildfire. He scored a fifty-four-yard touchdown and carried twenty-five times for 134 yards. He caught five passes for 62 yards and returned two kickoffs totaling 104 yards. At the final whistle, the Bears had trounced New Orleans 42-17, and Payton had clocked 300 total yards for one game, a single-game personal record that even he would never best.

Chicago's battered fans, steeled by a face-saving final win, began to believe. And Payton reciprocated. He'd dug in deeper and worked harder in one season than in all four years at Jackson. Even if he hadn't delivered a league title, he had delivered the message that the "Old, Old School Bronko Nagurski Bears" were back and on their way to becoming a force to be reckoned with in the NFL. The fans, the franchise and even the league sensed that something big was going to happen in Chicago. In the Second City itself, what Walter Payton did in the final game of his rookie year hinted at a glory road that lay just ahead. But for the rest of the country, the Bears' 1975 4-10 season was just the same as it ever was.

"Believe it or not, a lot of people didn't really start watching Payton until later in his career, in the eighties," says Bears old-timer flanker Johnny Morris. "Because when he came up, the Bears were a bad team. He had to literally carry that team. But people around the nation didn't really know about any of it. All they would see was a few highlights. A lot of the Bears' games weren't nationally televised, so a lot of people around the country never really saw Payton consistently, at his best game after game, until he was past his prime."

After the season was over, after the interviews, after the rubber chicken banquet circuit and the rest of the routines of the postseason, Payton returned to Mississippi, his family, friends and especially Connie, whom he married that summer. The lessons he'd learned in that first season drove him to work the Sand, run the Levee and pound the steps of the Jackson State stadium like never before. As training camp for his second season approached, Payton was in the best shape of his life.

The extraordinary strength, focus and commitment—the *physical and mental genius*—that Walter Payton brought to both his training regimen and his play, were borne of the simple and clear knowledge passed down from his father.

Walter knew with the matter-of-fact assurance of someone closely in touch with their natural gifts that his purpose in life was to use those gifts. He was *meant* to play pro football. Anything else would be a waste of his God-given ability. In the wake of his 1975 season, he now knew that he was meant to serve a larger purpose with the Bears. He would live his life, the life he now shared with Connie, and play the game that he played like no one else, in Chicago, for Chicago. If the Bears' hard-luck fans hadn't forgotten Payton's first "zero yards" game already, they soon would.

CHAPTER

04 Best Football Player Ever, Period

Since the time of David and Goliath and well through the Middle Ages, armies held one soldier above all others—this man was known as "the champion." Always an army's greatest warrior, this man was expected to lead on the field of battle, but he was also called to fight alone in single combat.

On the field of professional football, Walter Payton was Chicago's champion, always leading his team but often fighting through the lines alone. He was always able to surprise opponents with some unexpected reserve of ingenuity and aggression, always able to forestall defeat for his team when all effort appeared spent and all hope seemed lost. And like a Roman gladiator who survived in match after match, Payton was respected and feared by rival warriors throughout the NFL.

Warrior that he was, Payton adapted his enemy's tactics to his own use. In pro football's lexicon, dominant defenses blitz, cover and scheme while successful offenses shift, look for daylight and pass. Defenses invade while offenses evade.

But Walter Payton—by his own design—was the genius exception to the rule, a man with the brains and quicks to elude a defense, but the raw power and determination to attack and destroy it as well. Payton's one-hand pass receptions, his high-stepping backfield juking of the onrushing blitz and his uncanny instinct for protecting the ball were nimble offense play personified. But unlike so many of his running back peers, Payton didn't sidestep contact with fancy footwork or avoid a fight by running out-of-bounds if it moved his team a yard further downfield. Payton initiated combat by taking the ball straight down the field. He always thought north-south, not east-west.

And he didn't just hit back, he hit first. Walter Payton redefined his position's traditional punching-bag role by making a target out of those who would target him. He was a truly punishing piledriver who played running back the way you'd expect Dick Butkus or Lawrence Taylor to. And everyone in the league—offenses, but especially defenses—learned the hard way the second they walked onto Walter's field.

A little-known fact of life on any football team from high school to the NFL is the social separation between offensive players and defensive players. No man plays both ways on any one team. Players must choose a side of the ball to play early on in their football lives, and rarely do they switch affiliations. Defensive players choose defense because they love contact, and they view offensive players—from the quarterback all the way down to the lineman—as fearful inferiors. Offensive players, on the other hand, see their defensive teammates as a collection of hotheads incapable of executing a game plan or thinking beyond two or three yards—or seconds, for that matter—down the field. And from day one at training camps around the country, defenses talk trash and jaw about how their line of the ball is where the real men play.

Payton was one of the few Bears, if not the only one, who could walk both offensive and defensive ends of the locker room with impunity. No one said boo to Walter.

Simply put, Payton took the fight to the enemy. "Why should I be the only one who gets clobbered?" he asked. "I try to neutralize the other player's attack by attacking him. As long as there are two of us in on the play, the other guy ought to take half the blow. Then it won't hurt me so much. If you don't explode into him, by the laws of physics you're gonna take most of the impact."

Over thirteen seasons, Payton taught his theory of physics to hundreds of unwilling students. "The quarterback handed the ball off to Walter," recalls Cowboys nickelback Bill Bates of his first lesson from Walter Payton. "I'm right in the middle, and it's just me and Walter. I hit pretty hard and was known as a good tackler. Well, he hit me with his forearm right in the chest and in the shoulder. When he hit me, he knocked me off him and gained about another twenty-five yards. You always think of the defensive guys as hitters, but for him to be the one actually initiating the hit was something very extraordinary from a running back."

Thinking and running north-south first was both a matter of pride and a matter or strategic necessity for Payton. He understood the simple truth that most other running backs don't: every yard gained is a yard taken. And every yard taken from a defense saps its will. Giving ground rips the cockiness and confidence out of even the most ferocious of hitters. "I'd skip through the line, turning and digging and trying to accelerate," he said of his aggressive approach, "but when somebody cut off my route, I lowered both head and shoulder and drove into him. It usually resulted in a few more yards gained before I went down." No less an admirer than Jim Brown agrees. "He would fight you for every inch, all day long," Brown points out, "with no thought of trying to get away from a hit unless it was expedient to get away from a hit, no thought of running out-of-bounds." Payton would sooner give up the ball to his enemy than duck a potential yardage-gaining hit. "I'm not gonna run out-of-bounds before I hit somebody first," he would promise himself. "Why run out-of-bounds and die easy?" he reasoned with a warrior's pragmatism. "Make that linebacker pay. Make him earn your death."

Most players couldn't survive a scorched-earth field campaign like Payton's for a single year, let alone for thirteen seasons. But Payton's astonishing physical condition kept him off the disabled list for nearly his entire career. "The fact that Walter survived thirteen years in the league, missing only one game, especially with the beating that a running back takes," says '85 Super Bowl quarterback Jim McMahon, "is simply the most amazing stat. Shit, I've missed eight games a year. He took a lot of pounding, but he dished out a lot of pounding." When Payton's business partner Mike Lanigan asked Number Thirty-four how he'd remained uninjured for so many playing seasons, Payton chalked it up to his confrontational approach. "He said, 'Mike, it's because I used to hit them right before the contact. If you look at those tapes of me, in 99 percent of them I'm on my stomach at the end. I attacked the tackler.' That's why."

Payton's longevity was inexorably tied to the peak physical and mental conditioning he obsessively pursued throughout his life. "He was the strongest guy I ever met," says McMahon. "He was muscle everywhere." Payton's self-created training ritual had no equal. "I never understood the workout ethics and the philosophies of any other athlete I ever met," he once confessed— and it's not surprising. His preseason workouts on the Sand and the Levee in Mississippi and later on the Hill in Arlington Heights are deservedly the stuff of legend. "He had a regimen that defies what the U.S. Marines were doing,"

Mike Ditka says. Payton's career began in the days of straight-leg sit-ups and concluded in the era of ultrasound. Decades before trainers prescribed the Pose Method, stability training or core training, all common in the NFL today, Walter Payton achieved the incredible fitness base those techniques were designed for through his own remarkable off-season workouts. He didn't know the trendy names, but he intuited the programs before the physiologists had even thought of them. He knew the ordeal he had to put himself through in order to be his best.

On the Hill he bent into each punishing step. Over and over he pushed himself up the steep incline to develop a cadence and pace that gave him the sudden bursts of speed and instant changes in direction his gladiatorial arena demanded on flat ground. Running up on his toes in the Sand, Payton created an extraordinary synthesis of balance, strength and speed, coalescing his mind and his muscles into one. He burnished his natural running ability to the point that he moved, swiveled and shifted his weight with a dexterity and power that neutralized and deflected the force of any hit back onto an opposing player. NFL training camp was a chance to get in shape for many of his teammates, but for Payton it was just fine-tuning. "When I went to training camp," he said, "it was like a vacation. I trained harder in the off-season than I did during the season."

Jim Brown says of the champion who usurped his rushing crown, "When you take that strength and that striking power and that quickness and that balance and combine it with his intelligence, you have a total package." The intelligence and self-knowledge Payton brought to his game were truly exceptional. "I understood that I might not be the best; I understood I might not be the strongest; I understood that I might not have the speed," he explained. "But I figured if I took all of those qualities that I did have and put them all together, I had something no one else had." Mike Ditka puts it

a little differently: "There were guys who had more talent, but they didn't have the will to do what he did," Ditka explains. "His strength was his heart, because that's the way he played the game, with his heart. He willed himself to be what he became."

"The game of football is about 85 percent mental," Payton said. "Sure, you have to be able to physically play, but you have to deal with the losses and get yourself mentally ready to go back for another week. It is especially important to be mentally strong when you are on a team that struggles. It is difficult to stay consistently motivated when you are losing. That's when it is easy to slip, to give in for a moment. I was always fearful that I wasn't in the best shape I could be. I always wondered if I had slipped a little bit. That motivated me. It was why I made myself train so hard in the off-season." Connie Payton agrees. "Even through all those years when things weren't going well," she says, "his reaction was to work out that much harder, to train that much harder, so he could stay healthy and be even more productive."

Payton trained his body to take the incessant hits and constant physical punishment his opponents lived to dish out. And he trained his mind to think beyond the usual limits of how running backs were "supposed" to play the game. Former teammate and Tennessee Titan head coach Jeff Fisher recounts how Bears equipment manager Ray Earley gave him a surprising glimpse into Walter Payton's mental game: "'Here,' he said, while grabbing one of Walter's cleats, 'put your hands inside this shoe and feel around.' It was one of those Spot-bilt shoes that had inch-long, screw-in cleats on the bottom. I stuck my hand in the shoe and literally scratched and nicked my fingers. Walter had pulled out the insoles to his shoes so that, with his feet inside the shoes, he could actually feel the ends of the screws that attached the cleats to the bottom of his shoes from the other side. He did this so that he could always feel every cleat against the bottom of his feet, which he felt gave him great feel for maintaining traction while running on the turf."

Whether pounding his body on Astroturf-covered concrete, nimbly keeping step in muddy grass or refusing to yield on frozen ground (the hardest playing surface of all), Payton stole thousands of yards from eleven-man armies of defenders in all kinds of weather for thirteen straight seasons. And he did it in unpadded shoes with spikes that ground into him almost as much as they dug into the ground he ran. He needed the advantage of that contact. All he had to do was endure a little pain.

As the years rolled by and the hits kept coming, Payton steadfastly played through more and more pain. Fred Caito, who was on the Bears' training staff for years, saw the toll it exacted—and Payton's will to overcome it: "He played the game with broken ribs, a separated shoulder, severely sprained ankle and bad knees the whole second half of his career. He would fight through those things and get his treatments, and that's where his uniqueness was. He hurt, and he suffered, and he paid for it. Even when his rib was broken, he could play with it. He could twist and turn with bandages. That made him a rare, rare individual."

Later, fans marveled at the sleek, studied moves of great running-back dynamos like Barry Sanders, Emmitt Smith and Marshall Faulk, but Sweetness

remains the standard of true offense by which all who come after will forever be judged. Even injured, Payton was a one-man wrecking crew who wore down defensive lines without mercy.

And mercy was something he knew never to expect in return.

"Some of my friends around the league said teams actually started feeling sorry for me," he laughed. "I was a marked man. Everyone knew our offense was Walter right, Walter left, then Walter up the middle. And I knew everyone was gunning for me. You have to just keep playing." Former Green Bay Packers linebacker Rich Wingo remembers a 1979 game when the Packers tried to use their home ground itself to take down Walter Payton. "Walter was just kicking our butt—he was controlling the game," recalls Wingo. "We were playing at Lambeau Field, which has an underground heating system. It was freezing. I mean, it was bitter. And it was rainy—the field was real wet. So this assistant coach, who knew right where all of the switches were, shut down the field's heating system between the twenty- and thirty-yard lines in the Bears' end. The ground turned hard as a rock. Walter had a hard time keeping his feet after that." Hard time or not, Payton still gained 115 frigid yards and led the Bears to a tight 15-14 victory.

Payton's never-say-die approach to the game carried him past opposing defenders on every terrain and straight into the record books. In 1977, only his third year in the league, Payton rushed for an astonishing 275 yards on forty carries in a tough victory against the divisional archrival Minnesota Vikings.

"Probably the best individual performance day I ever had was when I set the single-game rushing record against Minnesota," he maintained. "It was like being in the zone. You know, everybody always talked about how Michael Jordan used to get in a zone. Michael was in the zone every time he got on the court. He was amazing. For me, there are times when you get

PAYTON RUSHES FOR 275 YARDS

1977 HIGHLIGHTS

3

Payton Rushes for 275 Yards

Chicago, Ill., Nov. 20, 1977. The sensational Walter Payton today rushed for a record 275 yards as the Bears defeated the Vikings, 10-7. Payton gained 144 yards in 26 carries in the first half. He rolled 58 yards to the Minnesota 9-yard line with less than 3 minutes to play and broke the mark in final 2 carries.

out on the football field and you never tire. Every time the play is called, you know exactly what you are supposed to do and you do it."

Incredibly, Payton's record for most rushing yards in a single game remained intact for over twenty-three years, until it was broken (by a mere three yards) in the 2000 season by Corey Dillon of the Cincinnati Bengals. But Payton wasn't done rewriting the record books.

On a chilly Sunday afternoon game at Soldier Field against the Saints in 1984 (his tenth NFL season), Payton vanquished a mighty gladiator he never battled face to face. He broke Jim Brown's all-time career record for rushing yards. In a first-ballot Hall of Fame career distinguished by ten individual NFL records and twenty-eight team records, Payton's all-time rushing title is the achievement most solidly linked to his name. Eclipsing Brown's mark of 12,312 yards was a huge sports milestone. As sportswriter Kevin Lamb wrote at the time, "This record was the big one, like Henry Aaron bearing down on Babe Ruth—only more so, because Payton had to outrace Franco Harris to get there first." As Payton drew close to Brown's record, the media was in a frenzy, and Bears fans held their breath right up to the moment the Bears and the Saints took the field.

What Payton did after the six-yard sweep play that put his name over Brown's in the record books says as much about the man as his record-setting achievement itself does. In characteristic fashion, Payton chose to deflect the attention away from himself so that he could simply get back to doing what he did best and pursue the thing that mattered far more to him than breaking records: winning each game and taking his team to the Super Bowl. Rick Telander observed in *Sports Illustrated* the week after the record had fallen, "When Payton's moment of glory came, he wanted the game to continue. He rose from the pile of New Orleans tacklers—linebacker Jim Kovach had hit him first—ready to run again."

Looking back, Payton himself simply explained, "We had momentum." The last thing he wanted was a swirl of hoopla to detract from the team's efforts that day. "I'm not like one of those game birds who shows his feathers to attract a mate. I'm not flamboyant," he said. As Telander noted, right before the Saints game Payton made a point of downplaying the significance of what everyone in the locker room knew would occur that day: "In the pregame warm-up, Payton told his teammates to forget about his impending record and just win the game." It summed up the essence of Payton: prevail against the opposing team. Take the prize you've come for—win the game. Compete.

Even when he was having fun, he never stopped competing. "Everything with him was a contest," recalls single-season Bears quarterback Rusty Lisch. "Who can punt the ball the farthest? Who can throw it the straightest?" During training camp the oppressive summer heat made most of the team find some shade and kick back during water breaks. "Not Walter," remembers Lisch. "He would run across the field to where there was a crowd watching and maybe grab a little kid out of the crowd and start running around the field with the kid, lifting him over his head as though he were lifting weights or whatever. You realized after a while that all this entertaining was another way for him to train. He was working out the whole time, whether it was lifting a kid over his head, like in weight training, or just continuing to run while everyone else was resting up."

Payton didn't just show his lighter side to his teammates. The Cowboys' Bill Bates remembers one surprising sack. "I tackled him one time," he

says, "got up and as I turned around, he pinched my butt. I turned around, and he just giggled." Matt Suhey feels Payton's sense of humor balanced his relentless on-field intensity. "He's got a tremendous ego on the field, but he also has a great sense of humor, an ability to say something light at the right time," he says. "When I dropped a pass against the Colts, on the way back to the huddle he said to me, 'You can always get a paper route or join the Army.' And he's a good imitator. He does a great Ditka and a great Buckwheat."

"Maybe it was just his makeup," Connie Payton recalls. "He was someone who has to be busy. And yeah, it would drive me a little crazy sometimes. I'd say, 'Enjoy life,' but for him, that was enjoying life." As a boy in Mississippi, Payton ran barefoot along the Pearl River with his brother and their friends. They played for the joy of playing. That child's sense of play got him into football as a teenager, where he learned to play a juking, dodging, head-first style that led him to college ball and on to the pros. It became a deadly serious business, but it was a business he loved. That love kept Payton young for his whole NFL career.

As the Greek philosopher Aristotle wrote, "Pleasure in the job puts perfection in the work." Payton's work was his pleasure. His play was perfection.

Ancient warriors trained in a single form of combat—the short sword, the bow and arrow, calvary—but football's greatest competitor, Walter Payton, excelled in every aspect of his chosen discipline. "There were so many other things he could do," says Payton's college teammate and

roommate Rodney Philips. "As a receiver coming out of the backfield or throwing the ball or carrying out a fake or chasing down the opponent on an interception or fumble, he did everything," says Mike Ditka. "If you ask other coaches around the league who watched Walter Payton block, they'd say he was the best blocker by far that they've ever seen at running back." In his thirteen seasons with the Bears, Payton not only played his own position better than anyone ever had before, he also was the Bears' backup punter and placekicker. He threw eight touchdown passes in his career and even started a 1984 game as the Bears' quarterback.

But perhaps the single core strength that made Walter Payton football gladiator supreme was the one that held all his skills together. "I think there was a heck of a lot more in Walter's mind than being the greatest back of all time," says Mike Singletary. "He was motivated by more than just being the best player." What motivated Walter Payton was a responsibility to his team, a belief that he was serving a greater purpose beyond himself by playing full out for that team. "The Bears are a team, and I'm just one guy," he once said, "but I'm one guy who will continue to strive for perfection as a runner, a blocker, a team player. There's nothing like being on a team, nothing. It made race and where we came from not matter." Payton sustained his excellence as a player with the justification of a man who understood that playing football was his purpose in life. Winning, being the best, was his humble responsibility to the ability he'd been blessed with. "My running ability is a God-given talent, and the worst thing I can do is waste it or not do all with it that I should," he said.

An NFL running back is lucky if his playing life lasts a decade. Payton shone for a decade and then some. But like the colosseum heroes of old, who rarely survived to middle age, Payton's life itself would be tragically

CHAPTER 05 | Super Bowl XX

The city of Chicago had been intimidated by Al Capone in the twenties and ruled by Richard E. Daley in the sixties and seventies, but it wasn't owned by one man outright until the eighties. In 1984, Chicago was Walter Payton's. The kings and emperors that shaped the destinies of ancient cities had always been dreamers. Walter Payton was no different. The dream he shared with his adopted city was a vision of victory against the rest of the NFL and against the tide of history itself. In 1984, Walter Payton could see the Bears' first Super Bowl win on the horizon.

Payton was thirty years old, in the best shape of his career and spearheading a Chicago team unlike the teams he'd carried in previous seasons. Eighty-three was a shakedown cruise. The season had started out rough, but Mike Ditka's revived and retooled Bears climbed out of the midseason basement with five wins in their last six games. All the new parts of the team, like quarterback Jim McMahon and defensive coordinator Buddy Ryan's 46 Defense, had been battle tested in the heat of competitive play. Looking ahead to 1984, veteran Walter Payton knew that at last he was on a team that could fulfill his nine-season dream of a Super Bowl ring.

- First Brown -

Chicago fans had been going back and forth through the wringer for decades. They'd rallied around great players like Johnny Morris, Dick Butkus, Gale Sayers and now Walter Payton, and they'd united in mourning for the fallen Brian Piccolo. For the last nine years, Da Fans had cheered Payton's charge through record season after record season, only to helplessly watch the Bears stumble in hard-luck defeats like a carelessly thrown away wild-card loss to Philadelphia in '79. They couldn't be blamed for being superstitious, even now that they had the best team anyone could remember. Chicago's fans searched for an omen. They needed a sign, and for once the sign was there. The timing was perfect. How could the year that Payton closed in on breaking Jim Brown's 12,312-yard rushing record not end in a trip to the Super Bowl, too? Chicago confidently buzzed about their team's postseason prospects while the entire country watched Walter Payton approach a parallel individual triumph.

Payton believed in dreaming big, and dreams didn't come much bigger than taking Jim Brown's title. The numbers were clear; this was the year that the title would fall, and Payton knew the rushing record was his for the taking. But with the momentum and unity the Bears were enjoying, Payton was of two minds about the crown he would surely be wearing by season's end. Caught in the media frenzy's headlights, he was tempted to look back over his shoulder to see if the contenders for the rushing prize, Earl Campbell, Tony Dorsett, John Riggins and especially Franco Harris, were gaining. But realistically, he needed to keep his focus and the Bears' focus on moving forward.

And title or no title, Payton was running wild. He was on his way to an eleven-touchdown season and would finish the year with 1,684 rushing yards; it was his best year since 1977 and the second best of his career. The

Bears had broken '84 wide open by trashing Tampa Bay, then shutting out Denver. The Denver game featured a spectacular fifty-plus-yard touchdown run from Payton. But Jim McMahon was sidelined, and the Bears' offense lost steam. They limped through the next few games so feebly that Payton's rushing title progress slowed to a walk. Facing Dallas, Payton needed 221 yards to unseat Brown. When he went 130 yards on twenty carries in the first half, the champagne was put on ice. But in the second half he only carried the ball five times. Chicago fell to Dallas 23-14, and Payton still needed another sixty-seven yards in order to make history.

The Bears walked out onto Soldier Field the following week, on October 7, sure that Payton would clinch the rushing title that day. Mindful of the media attention Payton and Harris's race had generated, the Bears organization originally planned a ceremony when Payton hit the magic number. But Payton refused. Record or not, it was only week six of the season, and the Bears needed to keep their eyes on the true postseason prize. It was a potential title year, and the team was at last really a team. Stopping play for speeches and handshakes was not how football games were won. "Forget the record," Payton told his teammates before the game. "We're going to win."

Midway through the third quarter it was Bears 13, New Orleans 7— Bears' ball, second and nine on Chicago's twenty-one-yard line. Jim McMahon, back off the disabled list, called the signals on a time-tested sweep play, Toss 28 Weak, that the offense could do in their sleep. McMahon took the snap and pitched out to Payton. Mark Bortz, Dennis McKinnon and Matt Suhey went into the hole. Payton danced back, found his spot, tucked and ran left toward the Saints' weak side. When the play ended, Payton had gained six yards. He was also now the leading all-time rusher in NFL history.

The game *did* stop. It had to. As Soldier Field went crazy, Payton poured on some additional hustle to outrun a group of charging photographers. He ran to the Saints' sideline to escape, took the opportunity to shake hands with New Orleans coach and former Houston Oilers legend Bum Phillips, then made his way back to his own side. The game ball was collected for display in the Pro Football Hall Of Fame, and per Payton's wishes, normal play resumed as quickly as possible. The Bears bested the Saints 20-7.

"When he broke the record he didn't say very much at all," Mike Ditka remembers. "It was really subtle. They stopped the game, gave him the ball, everybody gave him a standing ovation. I know that was something that he wanted to do, and I don't think after he did it that he thought it was the most important thing. I think he expected to do it."

Payton later downplayed his achievement as a momentary pause along the road to the Super Bowl. In fact, Payton said, "I don't believe I ever broke Jim Brown's record." Later he would remark, "I think it's still standing. I don't think the record books need to be rewritten. I didn't do it in the amount of time that Jim Brown did. If you can't do it in nine years and eight games, then you can't break his record. I had more games and I played longer, so I didn't break it."

In good times as in lean times, Payton kept his sense of humor. When President Reagan called from Air Force One to congratulate him, Payton answered the phone with, "The check's in the mail." The check was, in fact, on its way to the bank. The Bears gave Payton a $100,000 bonus, and a sponsor gave him a canary-yellow Lamborghini that he would use to terrify any teammate foolish enough to accept a ride.

Brown and Payton spoke by phone after the game. "Some people I would not have talked to because I would not have had that level of respect," Brown said. But #34 deserved the prizes, and, more importantly,

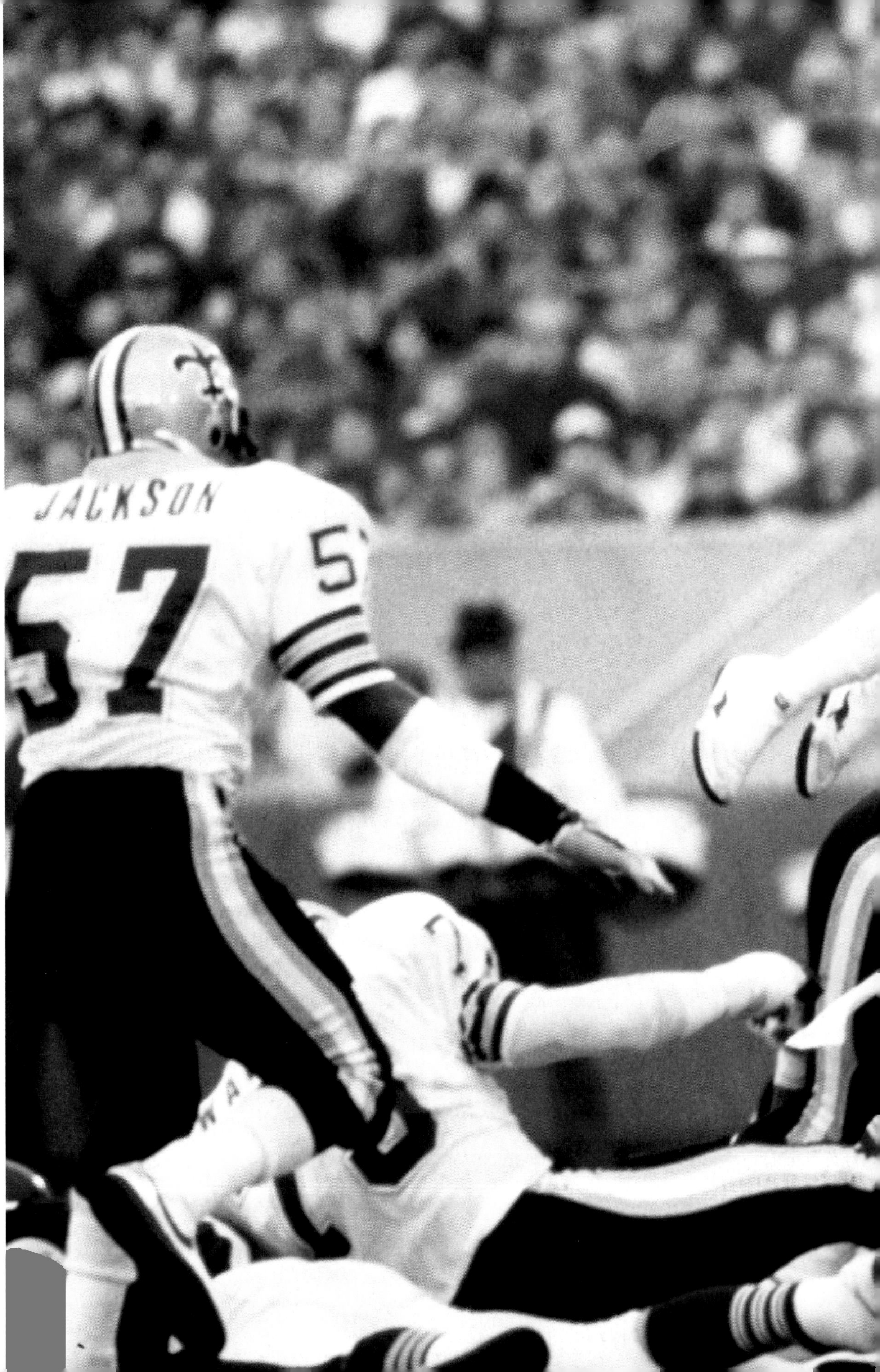
JACKSON
57

he shared the glory. Payton dedicated the record-breaking game to the memories of Brian Piccolo, Joe Delaney and David Overstreet, three players who died tragically before the age of 30.

- Wait Till Next Year -

The rest of the regular season campaign was costly but a success. McMahon went out again on a nasty kidney bruise. His replacement, Steve Fuller, was sidelined a few games later. After Fuller's substitute stumbled, Mike Ditka even tried putting Payton in at QB. But Sweetness only mustered a 20-14 loss to Green Bay. The Bears rallied and slapped down Detroit 30-13. So Chicago crossed over into postseason play for the first time in five years. The next wall they had to climb was at RFK Stadium—the powerhouse Washington Redskins.

For all the love his adopted city had for Payton, bad memories still died hard. "We hadn't won a playoff game since 1963," Payton recalled. "Nobody gave us a chance of winning that game, because we were playing on the road." The heavily favored Redskins took no chances. They did what every other defense had been doing for years and covered Payton with multiple shadows, no matter where he moved. "In the Washington game, they stacked the defense against Walter," Mike Ditka remembers. "I've never seen a guy run harder. He just ran harder and harder and got after them and stayed after them. They were cracking him with hits, too, you could hear it all over the stadium. Incredible collisions, and Walter would just get up and say, 'Hey, I'm coming right back at you.'" The Bears came right back and took the Skins, 23-19.

Chicago went wild. The Bears would be playing for a championship (NFC) for the first time since 1963. Now the city dared to dream of a football dynasty that would begin after their team vanquished Joe Montana and

the San Francisco 49ers at Candlestick Park. The Bears took the field inside the windswept 'Stick.

And choked.

There was no other way to describe the 23-0 loss that silenced Bears fans and badly bruised Walter Payton's ego. "The greatest feeling that I ever had in football and the worst feeling I ever had in football were a week apart," Payton later said. "I really believed that once we beat Washington we might go to the Super Bowl. I felt such a tremendous rush. I never felt such a rush in my whole life." The Bears had opened the door, then failed to cross the threshold. As the dejected team walked off the field, Wilbur Marshall came up to Payton and, echoing old Houston Oiler coach Bum Phillips, said, "Next year, we're not going to just knock on the door, we're going to kick the damn door down." Walter smiled but remembered that Phillips's Oilers never did vanquish their nemesis, the Pittsburgh Steelers.

- The Shuffle -

Training camp in Platteville, Wisconsin the following summer saw the Bears operating at a door-kicking level of confidence no one had ever seen before. Reporters and well-wishers overran practices. Jim McMahon sported a mohawk, and Chicago's '85 first-round draft pick, a gigantic defensive tackle from Clemson University nicknamed the Refrigerator, was getting pumped for quotes and photos. Chicago's Junkyard Dog defense was declared heir to the famed Monsters of the Midway defense of Dick Butkus's day. For the national sports media, it looked as if the Bears were the team to beat in '85. And for Chicago's championship-starved fans, it was almost too good to be true.

As always, Walter Payton used training camp to recharge his batteries after another impossibly grueling solo off-season workout schedule. Payton came down from the Hill in Arlington Heights mindful of the year 1985

could become. He knew he wasn't going to be working by himself anymore—he had a team that was ready to win. Payton was ready to play and ready to lead. "For so many years I was by myself, and then finally, for the first time, I had these guys saying, 'Hold on, I'm gonna lift this arm, and I'm gonna lift that arm, and I'm gonna help you up.' We all pulled together as a team. We all worked together. We were the perfect unit, and that is the reason. The myriad personalities were a perfect combination to just make it right. We all had mutual respect, and we all felt like every guy was giving 110 percent—every practice and every game."

In Payton's mind, the remaining hurdle the Bears needed to clear for the championship was simply a matter of focus. Payton had dreamed big and seen his dreams become a reality. The Bears as a team could do the same, but only if they shared that one vision as a team. As the season began, Payton's concentration narrowed and intensified. And it spread to his teammates. "During that season especially, I saw Walter having focus," Mike Singletary explains, "I think it was the season where he really began to vocalize and verbalize a little bit more of what he felt. For the first time, he began to speak, he began to talk in the huddle, he began to talk at practice and he began to talk before the game. 'Hey,' he'd say, 'let's go out there and do what we have to do.' I think everybody looked at him and said, 'Wow, this guy is really serious about this. This is it. We can really do it. Walter believes we can do it.'" Matt Suhey felt it too. "Walter helped that team feel free to express itself," he says. "Everyone felt that if Walter can do it, then I can let myself show a little."

They began 1985 with a come-from-behind win against Tampa Bay, then followed it up with a 20-7 win against the New England Patriots. Despite coming up nearly empty-handed in offense, the Pat's defense specialized in Walter Payton and held him to one of his worst rushing games

of the last few seasons. The Bears romped for their next six games and cleared the first half of '85 with a perfect 8-0 record. Payton and William "The Fridge" Perry (who was now being used by the Bears as a fullback in goal-line situations) formed an offensive symbiosis during the Bears' 23-7 pounding of Green Bay. When Ditka wasn't using Perry for short yardage breakthroughs, Payton was free to use him as a battering ram. Payton's power and Perry's size were a lethal combination.

In the second half, the Bears' momentum and the fans' postseason anticipation grew to outrageous proportions. Chicago slammed the Packers again, then bombarded the Lions, the Cowboys and the Falcons for a three-game combined 104-3 score. The Bears were a bona fide national sensation. Everywhere they went they were known by name. "That team was really a great group," remembers Connie Payton. "They were fun to watch and had so much personality and character. You just don't see that anymore. You fell in love with everyone on the team. They were all so much fun. It was amazing how it all kind of took off. They were America's team."

But the Bears hadn't gotten to the threshold of another Super Bowl on personality. The players all had grit to spare, and the coaches, Mike Ditka and defensive coordinator Buddy Ryan, were ace tacticians and stern taskmasters. It wasn't an easy road. In any season tension was a given, and in a winning season, with so much at stake, the pressure was relentless. But Payton, as always, kept the team's sights on winning, not on each other. "He wasn't just the best player on the field, he was the best leader off of it," remembers Matt Suhey. "That team would have exploded had there not been Walter there to keep it together, especially because there was friction from the coaching staff. All the chemicals were there for an explosion, and Walter proved he could instead turn it into the right mix. That was maybe his most important role on that team."

The Bears were riding high as they arrived in Miami on December 2 for a Monday night game. But third-year quarterback Dan Marino and the Dolphins invoked the spirit of '72, the year that Miami went undefeated, and robbed Chicago of an undefeated record. By the end of the night, the Bears were licking the wounds of their only loss of the season. It was a flashback to the Niners shutdown of the year before. That single loss angered Payton more than anything else, because he felt he'd relaxed and let his eye stray from the prize. "When I think back on that Super Bowl season, the first thing that comes to my mind is the loss to Miami," Payton said years later. "It was a loss that shouldn't have been. I think everybody on that team was praying the Dolphins would eventually get to the Super Bowl, because we had a score to settle."

One defeat couldn't rob the Bears of bragging rights. Any superstitious fear of cursing their postseason prospects by speaking of them outright was long gone. This wasn't baseball, and they weren't looking at a no-hitter. The Bears talked up the Super Bowl openly. And not only did they talk about it, they sang about it. The day after the discouraging Miami game, a handful of team members met to record a song for charity called "The Super Bowl Shuffle." In the video, the Bears shift their feet uneasily in the studio, like boys in an unfamiliar neighborhood, as they chant:

We are the Bears' shuffling crew.
Shufflin' on down, doing it for you.
We're not here to start no trouble,
We're just here to do the Super Bowl shuffle.

It was a sensation. "The Super Bowl Shuffle" made folk heroes out of the team and even charted in the Billboard Top Fifty. Payton loved it. "This

is the kind of stuff the guys do behind closed doors," Walter said to the cameraman. "In the bathroom when nobody's there, or in the house when everybody else is gone." In the video's outtakes, Sweetness clowned around and kissed McMahon on the cheek. A Soul Train veteran, Payton pulled rank and cheerfully declared Singletary's team choreography "third-grade level." Each featured Bear star took a verse. Walter Payton was first up, appropriately, and every word he sang was true.

> Well, they call me Sweetness, and I like to dance.
> Runnin' the ball is like makin' romance.
> We've had the goal since training camp
> To give Chicago a Super Bowl champ.
> And we're not doin' this because we're greedy;
> The Bears are doin' it to feed the needy.
> We didn't come here to look for trouble,
> We just came here to do the Super Bowl Shuffle.

Chicago killed the lights and went back on the offensive. They wiped out the Colts, the Jets and the Lions to finish the year 15-1. The Bears were in the playoffs with a bullet. Collectively, the team licked their chops at the prospect of hosting the Giants and Rams at Soldier Field. The Second City's team, "the Grabowskis" as Mike Ditka declared them in honor of Chicago's blue-collar roots, held New York to thirty-two yards on the ground and foiled 60 percent of Giants quarterback Phil Simms's pass attempts in a 21-0 shutout victory. The following week they performed the same surgery on Los Angeles, scoring on a Rams fumble in the final seconds to take the game 24-0. It was the first time in forty years that any League team scored two consecutive shutouts in postseason play.

Chicago's fans were looking forward to a Super Bowl rematch with the only team to beat the Bears all season. And Chicago's players were looking forward to sweet revenge. Dan Marino and the Dolphins were the ones to watch in the AFC playoffs, but it was not to be. Having secured the second and last wild-card spot in the playoffs, the underdog New England Patriots nailed an unthinkable three straight playoff victories on the road. The Pats' deliberate, running-heavy offense, strong special teams and keenly observant defense climactically chipped away at Miami, scoring seventeen points on turnovers, to make New England the 1985 AFC champs. The Bears were denied the contest they craved with perfect season spoilers Miami. It would be Bears versus Patriots in the Super Bowl in New Orleans.

- Game Time -

The carnival atmosphere that descended as the two teams converged on the Big Easy to practice the week before the game was unprecedented even by New Orleans standards. Chicago's rock-star swagger was a perfect fit for New Orleans, and the team partied late and trained early. Patriots guard Ron Wooten told reporters that a bear was a Russian mascot so New England was, therefore, playing against the Bears for the United States. Jim McMahon, who'd had no trouble generating headlines in the regular season, mooned the press. Through it all, Walter Payton remained what he'd been all season and for the nine seasons before—a stabilizing influence and the conscience of the team. It was a circus, but they were there to play under the big top on January 26, 1986. It would become a day of team triumph for the Bears that remains in the record books. And it would be a day of both pride and disappointment for Walter Payton.

On the second play of the game, it was Chicago's ball. McMahon called the wrong formation and sent Payton out with the ball but without any blocking. Payton was slammed by Pats linebacker Don Blackmon and lost the ball. New England recovered at Chicago's nineteen-yard line. The Patriots' quarterback Tony Eason tried to pass, but his open man tore a ligament reaching for the reception and had to be helped from the field. Two more passing attempts netted Eason absolutely nothing, and the Patriots kicked a field goal to get onto the scoreboard less than two minutes into the game. New England's passing offense remained a shambles for the entire game.

When Chicago regained possession, it became clear that New England's defense, notorious for peering into their opponent's backfield for any hints of the play to come, was there for one man and one man only. In the way they tracked him, shadowed him and followed him, the Pats' defensive

line seemed to think that Payton was the entire Chicago team. It was a repeat of their regular season matchup. When Payton moved, the entire Patriots defense swung with him like a pendulum. "The one play I remember—" McMahon said later, "the first play of the second half when we were backed up in the end zone—I faked the ball to Walter, and you could see the whole defensive football team go after him. I think that's really what hurt the New England Patriots in that game."

The Patriots' single-minded defense was a millstone for Payton but a strategic windfall for his team. Matt Suhey scored from eleven yards out as New England slammed the decoying Payton. With the Pats' defense swarming over Payton, McMahon had the game of his life with a nine-play, ninety-six-yard drive and a sixty-yard pass to Willie Gault that is still talked about in Chicago. As the score increased to 23-3 at the half, Mike Ditka emptied his bench and gave his second-string players a chance to shine. Even the Junkyard Dog defense got in on the carnage, scoring on an interception and a safety. The Bears cruised to a 46-10 win over the Pats.

But there was one very conspicuous exception to Chicago's scoring free-for-all. The team's beloved captain, their inspiration, their class cutup who had sweated, bled and led from the front every time, hadn't been given the opportunity to score a touchdown

himself. Payton was the Bears' sacrificial offering. He'd single-handedly distracted the Patriots' defense so completely—he still managed to gain sixty-one yards—that it freed up the rest of his team's offense to make Super Bowl XX the scoring freak show it became. By being the living legend that he was, by having taken the game to the Patriots and every other team the Bears had faced for a decade, Payton had sealed his fate. He was so good at his job that his opponents expended themselves trying to stop only him from doing it. By putting a muzzle on Payton, New England unleashed the rest of his team. Chicago's gladiator

willingly fell on his own sword, taking hit after hit after hit with the abiding dignity that he'd demonstrated for eleven straight years with the Bears. "I knew I was going to be a decoy today," Payton said after the game, "and I was prepared for it." His teammates were ensured a victory worthy of his sacrifice.

"It would have been great to score one," Payton later said. "In the days and weeks after the game, yes, I was bothered by it. But I was blessed to have parents who instilled in me that things happen for a reason. You may not understand it when it first happens, and it might not be something that you're going to be happy about, but down the line there will come a time when it will be shown to you."

Jim McMahon confessed, "On the touchdown that I scored, it was

a play designed for Walter, but the truth is I don't think anyone recognized it during the game. I know I didn't." Mike Ditka agreed. "I really didn't realize it. I never thought about the individual thing so much," he later admitted. "That was stupid on my part." Ditka's coaching intensity was notorious—he'd once broken his hand punching a blackboard to emphasize a point. He had been focusing on the game, on the win, not on the individual players. That was his job, and he got it done just as well as Payton got his own job done. But the omission of a Payton touchdown troubled Ditka for many years. "That was probably the most disturbing thing in my career. That killed me. If I had one thing to do over again, I would make sure Payton took the ball into the end zone. I loved him; I had great respect for him. The only thing that really ever hurt me was when he didn't score in the Super Bowl." McMahon harbors a similar feeling about Payton's scoreless day in New Orleans. "He had played for so long, and he had been the Chicago Bears for so many years," McMahon explains. "It hurt me not seeing him score a touchdown."

And even if late in the game Ditka had awoken from his win-at-all-costs trance and recognized his sentimental debt to Payton, Sweetness wouldn't have accepted charity. "I wouldn't have wanted anybody to have given me anything," he said when pressed to speculate about the late-game gesture that never materialized. "It would have been very shallow and hollow." If Payton harbored any hard feelings, he never showed it. "It didn't matter," he always maintained.

Sportswriters gossiped about William Perry's one-yard touchdown sideshow when the game was already out of reach. Some claimed that yard and that score should have been given to Payton. But there didn't appear to be any trace of animosity between the vet and the rookie. One of the first things that Payton did in the weeks after the Super Bowl was to record a duet, "Together," with the Fridge. And together, Payton and the Bears basked in the love Chicago had always had for them, even as hard-luck underdogs. Now the NFL's greatest fans cranked themselves up to a joyful fever pitch as their team returned home conquering heroes.

- Repeat? -

The Bears had made the Second City number one.

Heading into the 1986 season, the stage was set for complete Bears domination and a dynasty that might stretch into the next decade. The team made their mark in playoff history two years running and left a crater in Super Bowl lore that would never be filled. "The Super Bowl Shuffle" stars were all still there, and their chance at a repeat was little more than sixteen games away.

But it was not to be.

Everybody is an expert at explaining why. Some said it was because 1985 was a phenomenon—unique and short lived like a comet or an eclipse. Others blame the Bears' hard-luck tradition. Who could have known that Jim McMahon, who'd bounced back off the DL numerous times in '85, would be out for most of '86? Certainly not the untested Mike Tomczak, who'd struggle to fill McMahon's shoes. "When people ask me about it," the *Tribune*'s Don Pierson says of the Bears' no-repeat '86 season, "I always oversimplify things and say it was because they didn't have a healthy quarterback." Pierson recalls Walter Payton's reaction. "Payton said, 'Bullshit, it wasn't the quarterback at all,'" Pierson says. Payton "wasn't trying to cover up for anybody. He thought it was the downfall of the whole team, that everybody got selfish."

Like the rest of the team, Walter Payton had basked in the affection and adoration of Chicago's grateful fans after returning from New Orleans. He'd also made use of the opportunities the Bears' unprecedented superstardom offered. "The year after the Super Bowl, everyone had new endorsements, everyone had speaking deals," Payton said. But without games to win and single victories to share, the group's chemistry dissipated. "It really did change the team," he remembered. "When they came back, they wanted a bigger piece of the pie. You can only slice a pie up in so many ways. But for everybody to get an equal slice, everybody has to do their part. It didn't happen that way."

Payton had dreamed big and made it happen, first unseating Jim Brown's rushing title, then shepherding the brawling Bears to their Super Bowl success. The last big dream he had for the team was of a repeat like the Pittsburgh Steelers had enjoyed, twice. He could taste it; he knew it was possible. "It could have been us," he said without a hint of arrogance. "We should have done it. We were still good that next year, but we weren't the team we were in 1985. Because some of the hunger was gone—they tasted the forbidden fruit and it was good. "

Chicago did finish the '86 season with a 14-2 record, tied with the Giants for the best in the regular season. But the Bears fell short in the playoffs against Washington.

Walter Payton led the Bears up the toughest hill of all. He'd dared to dream of a triumphant win for the Bears and sacrificed his own glory to make that vision a reality. The Chicago Bears had achieved heights beyond even Payton's lofty expectations. But even Payton, who made pain the cornerstone of his training and his play, couldn't know how much the next few years would hurt. Not even he could've imagined how rough the team's tumble back down to earth would be.

CHAPTER 06 Running To Daylight

The team that had won Chicago's heart was slowly fading. The signs were there if you knew where to look for them.

The Bears that returned to Soldier Field in September of 1987 were not the team that had steamrolled the Patriots two years earlier. After Payton and the Bears beat the New York Giants in the season opener, things immediately started to slide. Jim McMahon got hurt again, and Mike Tomczk struggled.

Walter Payton was the unshakable spine in the team's anatomy. He had been for a decade. But he couldn't last forever, no matter how hard he fought the calendar. After twelve years in the league, his work ethic remained as strong as ever. But his body had aged. Maybe, just maybe, Payton didn't move quite as fast as he used to. Who could blame him? No player took more hits and complained less; few played with more pain game to game. If the Super Bears were back to just being the Bears, Payton, a nearly supernatural physical and leadership force, was suddenly almost mortal.

Despite finishing with a 14-2 record, 1986 was a disappointing season. There hadn't been a repeat, and there was no dynasty in the offing. "We had the same players we had the year before, but just not the same desire, the same hunger," Payton said years later. "We had every piece of the puzzle. But once you shake that puzzle up, it's hard to put it back together." One glorious year couldn't erase two decades of postseason no-shows. The ticker-tape euphoria was long gone. Mike Ditka would soon have to face lineup decisions that would have been unthinkable in 1985.

Nobody prodded Payton. At least not face to face. But when the Bears picked running back Neal Anderson in the first round of the 1986 draft, the hint was impossible to ignore. Aware that his remaining playing life could now be measured in single seasons, not decades, Payton eagerly signed his first $1 million contract for his next season in Chicago.

Ditka and the team worked with Payton to develop his strength and put more shoulder into his game. "He wasn't able to dart like he was earlier in his career," Ditka says. "He had lost the stuff, there's no question about it. He had to become more of a power runner. He had to really overpower people inside." Payton's closest friend and teammate Matt Suhey puts it more delicately: "I don't want to say he lost his step, but physically I think he had taken a beating over the years, and there's probably some people as good as he was at that point." For Payton, first was first and second was nobody. Maybe it was time for a bigger change.

Matt Suhey knew that a big part of Payton didn't want to hang up his cleats. "From the conversations we had then and afterwards," Suhey says, "I know he wasn't quite ready to retire. I think physically he could have played a couple more years. I don't know if he was ready mentally to retire." Mike Ditka remains philosophical about Payton's last season. "Focus changes," he offers. "Time changes individuals—it's just what happens. I knew that, and I knew how much it bothered Walter. It bothered me, because this is not the way you want people to go out."

The shadow of a players' strike had loomed over the season from opening day. And before the Bears could catch a break, the players' union hit a wall with NFL management and voted to walk out. Payton and his team were grounded on September 20 after two games. The relationship between Ditka and his players soured when the coach publicly sided with management. When the strike was called off four weeks later, the brotherhood forged in 1985 was over. Now the Bears were just showing up to do a job—they marched toward the playoffs without much enthusiasm or faith.

Most NFL vets picture retirement as a coach's whistle, an announcer's desk or a restaurant awning with their name on it. With his superstar profile, Payton discovered that he had other options. His agent, Bud Holmes, was tight with Bears general manager Jim Finks, and Finks was well connected to the NFL's administration. Finks knew that the league was concerned that there were no black team owners at that time. Would Payton be interested in correcting that? The matter of race in front-office football didn't really interest Payton one way or the other. He never made his skin color an issue in the way he played; why make it an issue in what he did off the field? But the opportunity to own part of an NFL team had his full attention. He had a choice: squeeze a few more seasons out of himself or quit now and try his luck on the other end of the game.

As the season neared its end, Payton made his decision. Maybe it was time for him to step up to the next level. He would have to leave earlier than he wanted, at age thirty-three, to grab for the brass ring Holmes, Finks and NFL commissioner Pete Rozelle dangled in front of him. The truth Payton couldn't admit to himself was that he was still torn. Looking back on his decision many years later, he regretted that he made his choice under the influence of the moneymen and the boardroom boys.

"I can tell you today," Payton once explained bitterly, "if it had been my choice, I wouldn't have retired. I would have definitely played more. I just kept saying, 'Two more years.' I was not ready to retire. I regret the fact that I listened to the counsel that was around me. Even in my last game, I had a great game. I was in incredible shape. I worked out all the time. I really, really felt that I could stay. But under the pressure of the people I chose to surround myself with, I was convinced that this was what I needed to do. So I didn't listen to myself; I didn't listen to my inner thoughts and how I really felt."

Matt Suhey, who understood how his friend felt better than anyone, still has a hard time talking about the broken promises made to Payton in his post-playing life. Payton took the advice of "people who weren't interested in looking out for him. A lot of the time, that's what he got." But for now everything was going according to plan. One more ring, then closing time.

On January 10, 1988, Chicago hosted the Redskins in a critical playoff game—all knew that the winner would have the inside track to the Super Bowl. It was a tight game the whole way, a classic playoff battle between the two powerhouse franchises of the eighties. As the clock ticked down, with Washington leading 21-17, the Bears drove downfield on the back of the man who had brought them to greatness. Payton took the ball eight yards short of a critical first down. Squaring his shoulders, he churned straight down the middle and leveled into the Redskin defense. An eight-and-a-half-yard, east-west seam leading out-of-bounds developed, but for Payton dashing out-of-bounds was not an option. It never had been. Walter Payton raged at the burgundy and gold wall collapsing on top of him, tearing at his opponents, fighting to break through. The game ended with Payton just inches short of a first down.

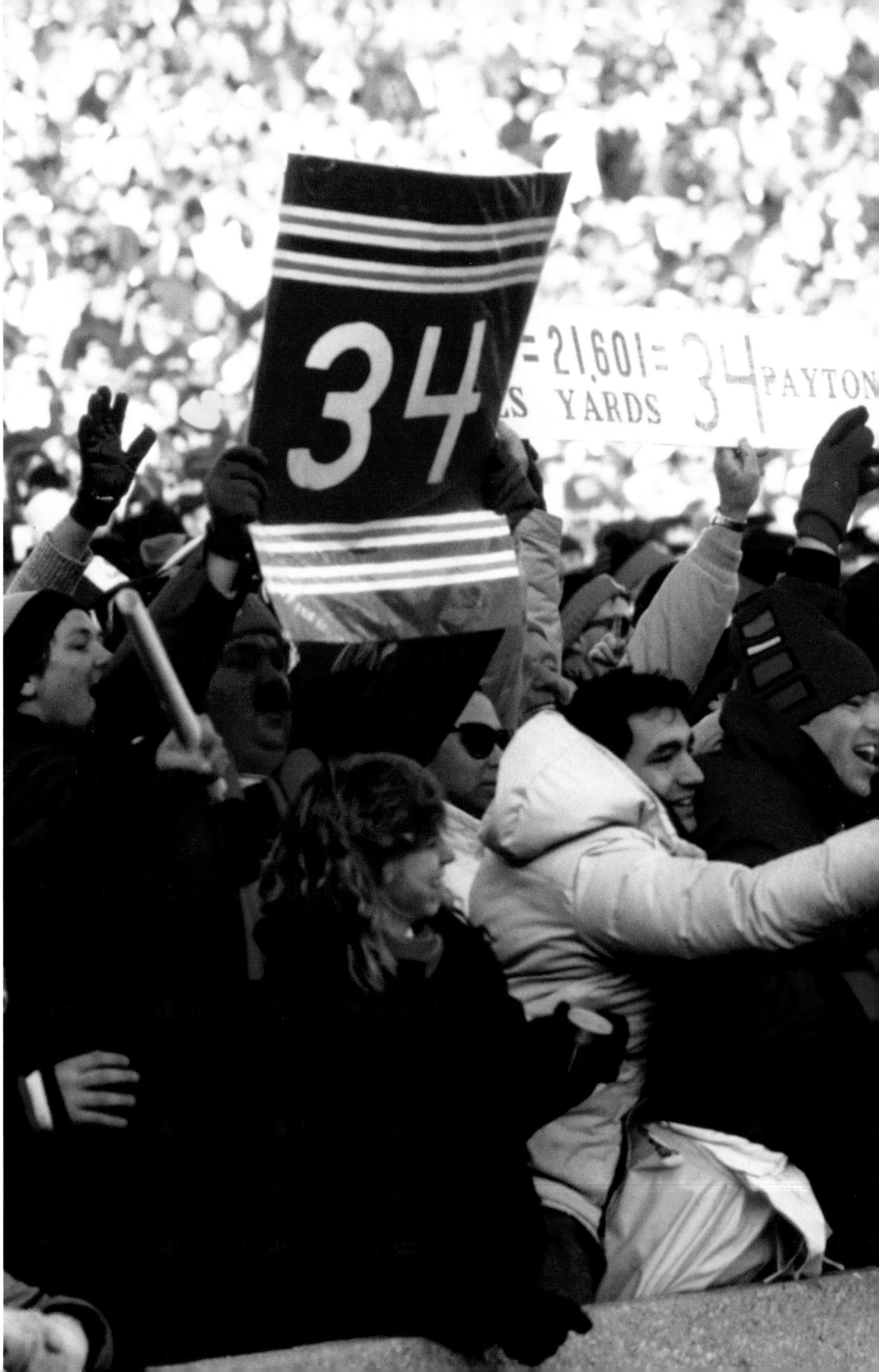
34
=21,601= 34 PAYTON
YARDS

Would he have made the extra yard five seasons before? It didn't matter. He gave it his all. The Bears watched the final seconds tick off of what would be Payton's last chance at another Super Bowl. Payton netted eighty-five yards on eighteen carries, and he received an ovation from Chicago's grateful fans that he would cherish for the rest of his life.

His farewell speech that day was as modest as his thirteen years of play were illustrious: "I came into this game because I loved to play," he said, "and because it was fun. It's still that way. Thank you for being here." Walter Payton was done. The fans cheered as his jersey was retired. No one would ever wear #34 for the Bears again. The bleachers and parking lots emptied. Cars jammed Lake Shore Drive for miles.

But Payton didn't leave the field.

Walter Payton sat alone on the bench, holding his helmet in his hands for what seemed an eternity. The game was over. But the 21-17 loss to the Skins was only a small part of what went through his mind and his heart in those moments. He stayed perfectly still, gently clinging to the memory of an on-field career that was now at an end—knowing that as soon as he left the sideline and walked into the clubhouse, things would never be the same. Years later, as he clung to life awaiting a liver transplant, Payton gave another reason for sitting there and breathing in everything about that moment. He was living his life to the fullest.

"Everybody said, 'Why did you sit there?'" Payton remembered. "'What were you thinking about? Why were you sitting there like that?' Think about it—we go through life so fast and so quickly. We miss so much. It's amazing. If you're driving to work every day, try being a passenger. Drive the same route that you drive every day, but instead of driving, feel the other side. I promise you, you will see things you have never seen before." He heard the cheers die, he felt the stadium empty and he saw thirteen years of excellence pass into memory. "That was my whole purpose—to sit there and just enjoy that moment. I would have sat there until they turned the lights off."

Connie worried that her husband wouldn't be able to adjust to his new life. He hadn't taken a break since the day he was born. "He didn't miss games, sit out hurt and know how to deal with not being part of a team. It was like going cold turkey," she recalls. "Here you are with all you've done; it's gonna be so different than for a lot of other people."

But Payton got busy right away. Apart from creating what would become the Walter and Connie Payton Foundation, Payton joined the Bears' board of directors, became a partner in a sports marketing company, was a founding director of a bank near his house in Arlington Heights, Illinois, and opened Walter Payton's Roundhouse, a huge restaurant and microbrewery complex, which was an instant success.

He went to the office every day, made public appearances, signed autographs and supervised his restaurant. But more than anything, he had his eye on the NFL ownership slot he had been encouraged to try for. The experience of owning a team seemed like the only thing that could come close to leading one. Walter Payton challenged himself as a matter of principle. What greater challenge was there than moving up from the gridiron to the front office? How could he lose?

The next three and a half years would be the most disappointing in his life.

Payton's agent, Bud Holmes, wasted no time meeting with investors for the prospective new teams. But Payton quickly discovered that since he didn't come with a war chest, the best he could hope for was a minority stake. The added value for any prospective teams was Payton's fame and personality. The Carolina Panthers offered Payton a minor interest in their team. But theirs was a small market, and Payton was disappointed that the

team's owners "wanted to keep leadership in the family," as they told him. He passed. Charlotte and Jacksonville briefly emerged as possibilities, but Payton took Holmes's advice and held out for something bigger.

An investor group from St. Louis looked especially promising. Financiers Jerry Clinton and Fran Murray, a part owner of the New England Patriots, liked Payton and were serious about his joining their St. Louis franchise team. Multimillionaire St. Louis businessman James Orthwein, (later to take controlling interest of the New England Patriots), agreed to throw in. Things were lining up nicely. It looked as if the team ownership that had lured Payton into quitting the game he loved might be for real. Then things got sticky.

In order to come together quickly, the St. Louis deal needed support from the local blue-blooded banker community. If Payton was nervous, he didn't show it. He was brought on board to act as a trustworthy, press-friendly face. As a veteran player used to dealing with reporters every working day of his career, Payton did what he could—he went on an all-out PR offensive.

"PAYTON'S RUNNING TO DAYLIGHT," trumpeted a 1989 headline from the **St. Louis Sun**. The accompanying article featured a large picture of Payton leaning toward the camera to make his point. "I think owning a team would be as exciting as scoring touchdowns," Payton is quoted as telling the reporter," but we're not just trying to fill our own pockets. This will benefit the whole community, area and state. With the desire that we have to do this the right way, all people will benefit." He wasn't just trying to sell the St. Louis consortium to the fans, he believed every word he said.

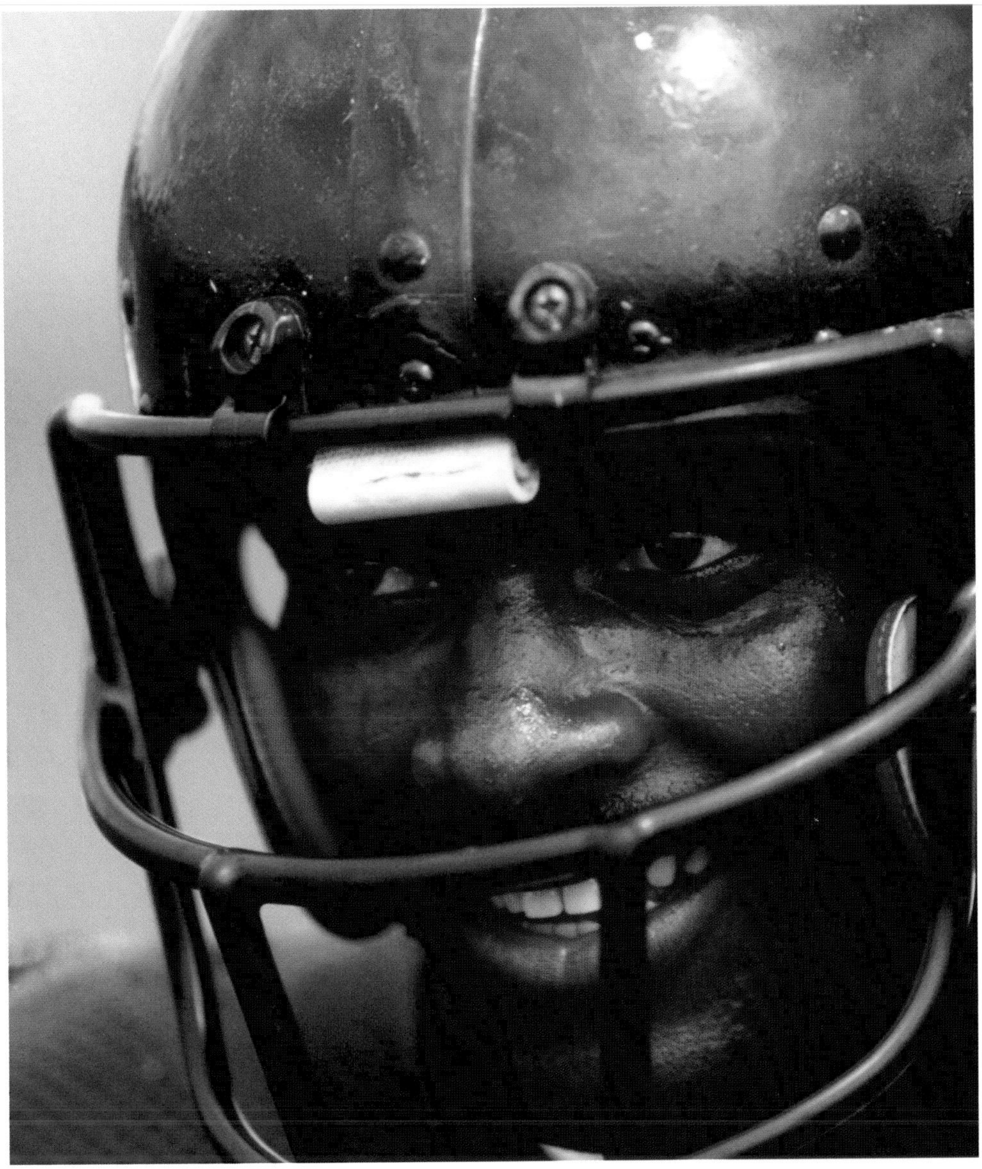

He also believed that the endorsement he had from Pete Rozelle would win the NFL over.

Apart from a few words from ex-Hilton executive James Sheerin, who had also taken a stake in the bid for St. Louis, none of Payton's main partners were quoted or even named in the article. Seen in hindsight, Payton's statements were a prayer, not a reflection of how the deal was progressing. Things were rapidly coming apart at the football seams.

Payton and the other board members agreed to meet that October to finally hash out the bid they would need to present to the NFL for consideration. Shortly before the scheduled meeting, however, friction between partners Jerry Clinton and Jim Orthwein came to a head. According to Payton, Clinton resented Orthwein's taking control and wanted Orthwein out. But Orthwein's purse represented most of the actual capital the group needed.

Always the peacemaker, Payton recalled telling them, "'Guys, I think we all have a common goal, which is to get this team.'" He stayed focused. "My whole position was 'Let's get the team and squabble later.'" But the infighting continued. And the whole process had gone on so long that Pete Rozelle, Payton's reliable champion at the NFL, was now within months of stepping down as commissioner. The clock was running out. There were plenty of other competing groups that were solidly financed and had prepared their bids without any internal strife.

NFL executives met to hear and review the various franchise bids that had been prepared. But the acrimony within the St. Louis group spilled out in their presentation to the league. "It was at the Hyatt right here at O'Hare," Payton remembered. "We did our presentation, and when the lead guys from the NFL came in, they said, 'You know what, guys? Get this stuff together. This is ridiculous. You're there if you can cut the squabbling.'" Payton and his quarrelsome crew were given a month to come back to the NFL with a unified presentation. But it was already too late. Ultimately, the league awarded a franchise to Carolina, the first team Payton had turned down.

The game ended. Walter's last hope was gone—lost to almost four years of constant struggle and campaigning on behalf of a team that could not hang together. After four years of work it was zero yards, maybe even thrown for a loss. He had nothing to show for his time or his effort. The St. Louis dream never materialized. Payton was happy to see former Kansas City Chiefs player Deron Cherry become the first black man to claim team ownership shortly thereafter (for Jacksonville, another franchise Payton had turned down), but Payton's professional football management life lay in disarray. His sure thing hadn't panned out. He'd lent his name, his reputation and his fame to a phantom.

"I couldn't believe it," Payton recalled. "I was so sure of it. There were business offers that I turned down because I was sure I was going to be in the NFL. That was going to be my full-time focus. It would have been my baby, no question. Those business opportunities that came to me right after I retired never really came back. Four years after retiring, I wasn't as hot. Others stepped in and took my place."

And he also resented his agent, Bud Holmes, for talking him into retiring while he still had some heat left. "No question," said Payton. "We haven't talked in a long time. I definitely have had a hard time forgetting the decisions I was asked to make."

Franchise hopes dead and buried, Payton still went to the office each day—returning phone calls, opening mail and checking in—but he'd lost something precious. What followed was a period when he was searching for the focus that had driven him through thirteen years without a single serious injury. His executive assistant at the time, tried to keep his spirits up, but Payton was withdrawn and sullen. "That was a sad time for Walter," she recalls, "just trying to find himself. It was a long stint." But then, slowly, Payton started coming back to life.

The one person who probably helped him the most was Mike Lanigan, with whom Payton founded the heavy-equipment company Payton Power. In fact, a large part of the Payton estate was made when Payton Power sold at a substantial profit. "For a guy who was so confrontational on the field and beat your brains out," Mike Lanigan remembers, "he was such a gentle, nonconfrontational person off the field. It was like two different personalities. Once you made it into his circle, he never did any due diligence on people that he dealt with—that's the simple Chicago South Side way of saying it. He didn't want to hurt anyone's feelings."

People took advantage of Payton's good nature, and that's putting it mildly. Payton had fun as an owner of CART—the Championship Auto Racing Teams—but it became yet another business venture that brought him friction instead of income. In the last year of Payton's life, he sued both his former business manager and CART racing partner to recover money he felt hadn't been paid out to him. Off the field, the trust Payton gave was rarely returned in good faith. Connie once said, "He believed you ought to be able to do business on a handshake basis. Unfortunately, not all of Walter's business partners felt that way."

Payton loved racing his Indy cars. Movie star and racing fanatic Paul Newman recruited Payton to race for the Newman racing team, where he quickly advanced to the Trans-Am series. But like many things Payton loved, this almost killed him, too. During a turn on the track up at Elkhart Lake, Wisconsin, his car flipped over, flew off the track and caught fire. Payton escaped with only minor injuries.

Years later, as his life drew to its close, Payton looked at the larger picture of fame, risk, failure and success. "We are all dealt blows," he said of the bumpy road he hit after retirement. "Reacting positively is what we have to do." Looking back on both his racing and his financial experiences, Payton admitted that unlike in the game of football, in the game of life, "I was often not in control."

But Payton's own body, that constant by which he'd measured his ability to handle anything life threw at him, was itself getting ready to betray him. Even as he filled his waking hours with everything from administering his foundation to racing any car he could get his hands on, he was ignoring pain as he had so often in his playing career. He still worked out like he had never left the game, and so he looked as strong and as healthy as he had in his heyday. But his constant stomach pains grew worse. He was guzzling Maalox. Inside him, something dark was slowly growing. Payton, the relentless optimist whose willpower had conquered nearly anything in his way, would shortly face an uphill battle not even his deep strength and profound faith could win.

CHAPTER 07 | Never Die Easy

By the summer of 1998, the swigs of Pepto-Bismol Walter Payton had incorporated into his daily routine no longer helped.

Something was wrong. Occasional stomachaches now came with more frequency. Foods tasted bland. The smell of aftershaves he had liked suddenly irritated him. Later, Walter would recall that he "felt a gradual progression of fatigue and just an overall sense of feeling lousy."

When he finally did see a doctor, he was diagnosed with "vitamin toxicity." Tragically, it was not the first mistake doctors had made. In the early 1990s, when Walter underwent routine medical checkups in preparation to race Indy cars, his doctors had found unnaturally high levels of enzyme in his liver. But nothing was done at the time.

In December of 1998, Walter reached out to Matt Suhey. Although they hadn't seen much of each other since Walter's retirement back in 1987, it was certainly in character for Walter to contact Suhey—friend, teammate and confidant, a guy who had literally blocked for him and remained loyal since the early 1980s. It was Matt Suhey alone who accompanied Walter on his very first trip to the Mayo Clinic for tests.

Walter was diagnosed with a rare form of liver disease known as primary sclerosing cholangitis, or PSC. The disease causes the body to assault its own tissue. In Walter's case, it had caused scarring of the ducts carrying bile away from the liver. The cause was unknown. And there was no known cure. Walter would die in less than two years unless he received a liver transplant.

Suhey remembers, "I went to the hospital, or I'd take him. And we checked him in under other names so no one would know he was there. He wanted to fight it by himself, and I think he had every right to do that. That's the way he wanted it. So I was going to uphold that." Payton, with Suhey in tow, returned for more and more tests. And waited.

Incredibly, the news got worse. In addition to the PSC, Walter also had cancer. And it was spreading. He began chemotherapy treatments immediately. Between the PSC and the cancer, Walter was in for the fight of his life. One can only imagine his mindset; in his quiet moments, he must have thought that if toughness, strength of will, faith and humility entered into it, then he would come out on the other side. No matter how steep, no matter how tortuous the incline, if only Walter could strap on the right helmet and get to work… it was just another hill. And there was no hill that Walter Payton couldn't run.

On February 2, 1999, this classiest of athletes and most dignified of men stepped up to the microphone to tell the world what was already painfully obvious. Having lost at least forty pounds, his visage gaunt and hollow, Walter stood before the assembled press corps in Carlucci's Restaurant and made public his very private battle.

"I felt this was nobody's business," Walter remembered shortly after the press conference. "Why couldn't this be a personal fight? Everyone was telling me the same thing about needing to make things public. They said I had to do it because it wasn't fair; it wasn't fair to myself, and it wasn't fair

to my family. People were starting to think it was AIDS or whatever, so my staff really sat down with me and said, 'Walter, listen, this has to be addressed.'"

Connie, too, knew something had to be done before the rumors spun out of control. Even if Walter wanted his privacy, she said, "'You're not any ol' body, and you're out in public, and people know you and they know the size you are. And they know the size you were. And they know something was up when they saw you go from 210 pounds, or whatever, down to 180-something.' I told him, 'Sure, I wish we could just live this and do it ourselves, but we can't, we can't.'"

The press corps erupted with questions. Most were respectful. Some were not.

"Am I scared?" Walter famously replied when a reporter asked him if he was. "Hell yeah, I'm scared. Wouldn't you be scared?" He held it together until Jarrett hugged him tightly. Then Walter lowered his head, weeping as he covered his face with an oversized microphone. Several reporters wept, too.

At the end of the press conference, with most of the attendants in stunned silence, one journalist asked Walter if he wanted to say anything to the Chicago fans. "To the people that really care about me, just continue to pray," he said. "And for those who are gonna say what they want to say, may God be with you also." Walter was referencing an incident that had occurred at an event on January 29 to celebrate Jarrett's decision to attend the University of Miami the following year.

Local WMAQ-TV sports reporter Mark Giangreco, now with ABC 7 News in Chicago, had covered the event. As the footage rolled that night in homes all over the city, he remarked to viewers that the sallow Payton "looks like Gandhi." The Payton family was aghast when they saw it, too. Walter's daughter Brittney, then eight years old, told her father it was "mean." And he could only agree, so he decided to put a stop to it by going public. Walter, who later said he'd made up with Giangreco, added that "the town could have had a modern-day lynching with Mark" for ridiculing Chicago's most beloved athlete.

Upon hearing the news of his illness, the public outpouring of love for Walter was immediate and unconditional, especially from the kids. An employee from the Walter Payton Foundation recalls that her ten-year-old nephew was devastated when he saw Payton on TV. "He was very upset that I hadn't told him Walter was sick," she recalls. "He looked at Walter as a father figure and told me he had a solution to the problem; he would give Walter his liver. I proceeded to tell him that he couldn't live without his liver. He said, 'It doesn't matter; Walter means so much to so many people. I am only ten years old, and the world would not miss me, but it will miss Walter.' I said that he couldn't give Walter his liver, and he started crying hysterically."

John Gamauf, a president at Bridgestone/Firestone, was amazed to get a call from his old racing buddy just days after the press conference. Walter was asking if he could come and do a speaking engagement. "He called me and he said, 'Gam, I just do not want to sit around the house,'" Gamauf recalls. "'But I would love to continue speaking to your customers as I do with you, because it's so enjoyable for me.'"

What followed was a flurry of pit stops, where the rapidly declining Walter would keep his spirits up by addressing tire customers: New York,

Cincinnati, Philadelphia, South Bend. Sometimes he was so sick getting out of the private jet that Gamauf had arranged for him that he could barely move off the tarmac. When Gamauf would ask why he bothered coming, Walter answered, "Because I made a commitment, and I really want to do this." So before each appearance, Walter would lie down, rest briefly and then turn on the charm like it was still the old days.

Walter also appeared on all the major talk shows: *Oprah*, *CBS This Morning* and *Larry King*, not just to tell everyone what had happened to him, but also to raise awareness about the rare liver disease. Walter, who had worked with kids through the Halas/Payton Foundation for years, found something else he could be proactive about. Involved in raising public consciousness, Walter became a staunch advocate of organ donation.

During this time, the Payton household and Walter's office tried to be as supportive as possible, but even with Walter's relentlessly upbeat attitude, things grew worse. Mark Alberts, who is still involved with the Walter Payton Roundhouse Complex in Chicago, remembers, "We always talked positively, thinking positive thoughts, not even entertaining the possibility that Walter wouldn't make it. If anyone could beat the odds, Walter could." Alberts also held reporters at bay as the wall of silence around the family grew steadily higher.

If the cancer didn't spread any further, doctors said, there was still a chance a new liver would work. But then Dr. Greg Gores, who had attended to Walter at the Mayo Clinic, came back in mid-May with the results of the latest surgery. There was no hope left. The cancer had spread to the lymph

nodes, which meant it was now a question of months, not years. Walter, characteristically, took the news in stride, keeping his appointments even as they, too, began to dwindle.

Just after noon on November 1, 1999, some of Walter's teammates sensed that he had died. "Toward the end, even at the time of his death, no one knew," says former Bears teammate Roland Harper. "I knew. I was there. I didn't go inside the house, I was outside. But I knew. It was mental telepathy, and I could just feel it."

A quiet service was held in South Barrington, Illinois, close to the Payton home. The Life Changers International Church displayed a color portrait of Walter before the altar that Walter had been given as a gift when he retired. The famous grin, underneath a headband, beamed out at the celebrants. Ditka was there. So were most of the '85 Bears, along with NFL commissioner Paul Tagliabue.

Five people spoke at Walter's casket: his son, Jarrett, his brother Eddie, NFL icon John Madden, Mike Singletary and Ditka.

Big Mike Singletary captured Walter's attitude of staying in the moment rather than focusing on the negative. He looked out at the sea of teary faces and said the counterintuitive thing, and it resonated. "I have to take a step back, and I have to give you the messages that I think he would want you to hear," he said. "The first one would be this: this is a celebration. And I think as he looks down, I think he's saying, 'Hold everything. Don't you understand what just took place? I am here on holy ground, and I'm running hills, man. I never thought I could run. I'm running clouds and stars and I'm on the moon! Wow!'"

And as Singletary's testimonial neared its end, he put into words as nobody else had that day how rare, how uniquely brave, his friend's final offensive had been. Because what Walter had accomplished from the time

he was diagnosed to the time he let go was a feat far greater than 16,736 yards. He had not given up hope. He never surrendered himself to a despair that surely would have swallowed up most others in his circumstances.

The big man with his horn-rimmed glasses looked out at the audience. "I want to tell you this: Walter made one last great run. Fourth down, no time-outs and he looked across the line of scrimmage and they were all there. He didn't have any blocking whatsoever. And as he looked, they were there to take him out. Hate, fear, unforgiveness, selfishness, everything else that you can imagine, they were there. And Walter was asking the question, how do I get past this? And as he looked forward, he just looked up, and Christ was there saying, 'Walter, touch my hand. Grace is yours today.' And Walter took His hand. He didn't have to run, he didn't have to jump, he didn't have to earn it. He was free."

CHAPTER 08 | Clearing The Path

Matt Suhey is still protective of his late best friend.

Because Matt's role in his professional life had always been to block the onslaught on Walter Payton, he is hesitant to speak with anyone or say anything about the man. But Suhey's quiet reverence for and loyalty to Payton is clear no matter how little he says.

Suhey is forty-seven years old. His body reveals that he is getting further and further away from his glory days on the field. But he still moves like a football player. He walks with a slight hunch, takes small steps with his center of gravity focused around his hips, as though he is still ready to take a hit from his opponent at any time.

When Suhey joined the Bears, Payton was already a legend. Payton had been making winning plays with fullback Roland Harper for five years. But in 1980, Harper's knees began to give out. Harper's ability to respond to Payton's unpredictable moves was key to winning for the Bears. While the team was on the cusp of success, it still hadn't reached that coveted championship. The Bears needed to find a replacement for Harper—and fast.

The replacement, Matt Suhey, could not have been more different from Harper, or from Payton himself, for that matter.

The Bears scouted Suhey when he was twenty-two years old. He had graduated from Penn State that year and could not have been more white bread, more massive or more Catholic. He was a third-generation Nittany Lion and the second-round draft choice that year. Suhey was already aware of Payton's reputation. "You heard a lot about him," Matt remembers, "but you didn't know much about him."

Unlike Payton, a starting backfield position was Suhey's to lose.

"Our lives were completely different," Matt recounts. "I came from a college, an academic atmosphere. Born and raised at Penn State, with six brothers and sisters, my grandfather, everybody came from Penn State. Joe Paterno was my sister's godfather. My grandfather coached at Penn State and played against George Halas in the National Football League—he coached my father. My father married the coach's daughter."

However, Payton and Suhey were alike in more important ways, despite their divergent backgrounds. Neither ever took the game for granted. And both had incredible thresholds for pain.

"I think everybody at the time felt that the money was very, very good and that you had to play hurt," Matt remembers of a different time in the NFL. "Because someone else was gonna step in there, and you'd never get your job back. I feel very strongly about that, even if I didn't like the times I got bumped up and hit. You had an obligation to the team and to the city." However, Suhey is still amazed by Payton's ability to play through pain: "And Walter played through some stuff that I never would have played through."

The respect Payton and Suhey had for one another would underscore their performance on the field and their friendship off the field.

"My locker was next to his," Matt offers to describe their early days together, characteristically downplaying his own role for the Bears. "My first year, I didn't play very much. Roland Harper was still there, a super guy. But he hurt his knee. And Dave Williams broke his leg." Because so many players were injured, Suhey quickly moved into the starting backfield. After that, the Bears would come to rely on Matt, who at five foot eleven refers to himself as "a short white guy."

At the start of Suhey's second season with the Bears, a 16-9 loss to Green Bay made Matt intensify his efforts to do better. After their next game, another loss in San Francisco, he decided to meet up with some friends to boost his spirits. As he was leaving the stadium, a voice stopped him: "Hey, where are you going?" It was Walter. "I said, 'Just going out to get something to eat,'" Matt recalls. "The next thing you know, it was 'I'll go with you.'"

The rest of the team had been waiting to see whether the Payton-Suhey combination would be a success. They wondered how Payton would interact with a player whose young football career and family background were different than his own. Also, as Harper's successor, Suhey was under serious pressure from the beginning. Luckily, despite different styles, Suhey and Payton connected on the field.

"When you've got the guy right in front of you," describes Harper, "there's this telepathy that goes on that connects you. And Walter liked people he didn't have to say a lot to. He liked people who just knew what he was thinking or where he was going. That overcame all the differences between Walter and Matt, because Matt grew to the point that he just knew Walter's thoughts."

Once again, Payton had defied color boundaries, and he did so in the racially charged atmosphere of politically volatile Chicago. "We were Ebony

and Ivory before Stevie Wonder and Paul McCartney," Walter once claimed. "I think our relationship really helped break down a lot of lines, a lot of racial lines, on the team and, some said, in the city. Here were two guys who just had to have each other, and everything just clicked. Remember, I came from an all-black college in the Deep South. Matt was one of the first white guys I really got to know. He knew I was nervous about all that, and he broke the ice by joking around all the time about it."

Matt quickly became close with Walter. Harper was right—their natural communication on the field allowed the fiercely private Payton to form a close friendship with Suhey. Payton had picked one more person—in addition to Connie—to let into an incredibly tight-knit circle of trust.

Perhaps they got along so well because Suhey understood Walter's boundaries with people. Matt knew where Walter drew the line in terms of getting close to people, which is why, according to Suhey, he was only "close to one or two people." Payton kept a divider between his public and personal lives. While he was great with his fans and would stop on his commute to Soldier Field to talk with a fan, he was not a social man. Or, as Suhey claims, he simply "wasn't always the most vocal." Also, while Walter famously loved to play pranks on his friends or teammates, Matt says, "People didn't play any pranks on him."

But Walter's persona was entirely one-dimensional when he was playing. He became forceful and relentless during the games. And though a man of few words, he could always communicate with Suhey to execute winning plays. And he just hated when a play didn't work out.

"Physically, on the football field, he never wanted to be embarrassed," Suhey explains. "He never wanted to play poorly, he felt very strongly about that. If he fumbled, you could always rest assured he'd be ready to make the next play. He took extreme pride in that. He had a tremendous ego when it came to playing football, and I say that in a positive way. He'd never embarrass his work ethic."

Payton's ethic showed in every aspect of his career. He played all but one game. Even if he was experiencing excruciating pain, Payton simply played through it. Suhey remembers a particular away game against the Dallas Cowboys during the Bears' winning '85 season.

"He'd hurt his ribs, and I would have gotten it numbed, but he would never take a shot—he'd just play with it," Suhey recounts. "He was down, and I looked over at him and noticed that his lip was quivering he was in so much pain, and I said 'What's wrong?' He wasn't getting up. He said, 'Help me up,' so I did, and I said to him, 'You gotta get out of here,' but he said no, and he continued to play. I would have been out, no question."

The Bears grew to become one of the best teams in the NFL. Walter became a superstar, and he only grew closer to Suhey. Because of Walter's shyness, Suhey would often be approached by their teammates with questions for Walter. If Walter was in a bad mood, people wouldn't ask him directly—they would go to Suhey. "People would come to me and ask, 'What's going on with Walter?' Or something like that. He wasn't always one to open up, even if he was friendly with everybody." Payton's private personality never meant he was rude. He would go out of his way to be friendly with his teammates and fans. "He had a special gift for that, for making people feel comfortable," says Suhey. "Joking around with waiters, giving those people the time of day. That was a great quality, and something I learned from him. But when you got him one on one, to get close to him was difficult."

Matt was not put off by Walter's shyness or his stardom. Matt wouldn't bite his tongue or hold back with his closest friend. Connie thinks Suhey's uninhibited attitude was probably what made them such good friends. "A lot of people said that if Walter didn't call them that meant he was too busy, so they didn't want to disturb him," she says. "Matt knew better. Matt would just drop by. And sometimes with Walter, that's how you have

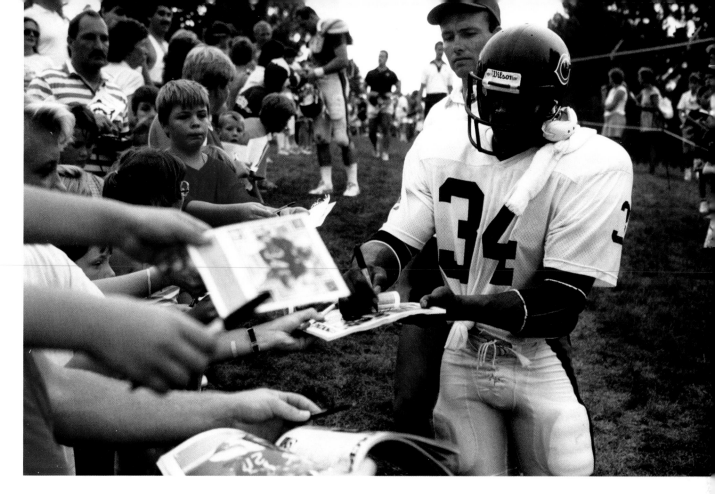

to be; you just have to do it. As forceful as he was in football, in his personal life Walter liked people sometimes to just take the lead role. That was Matt and me. We both understood Walter."

But in 1987, Matt's relationship with Walter changed forever. Walter retired, and Suhey, along with millions of Americans, was upset.

"It was disappointing, because he was still playing at a very high level," Suhey says. "It was such a bad way to go, because we had a great team, and I felt we were a better team than the Redskins. I knew we could win eight out of ten games. It was really a sad way for him to leave." Suhey also regrets that Payton was never able to fulfill his dream of becoming the first black NFL owner.

Leaving the NFL was probably one of the hardest decisions Payton ever made. But once the decision was made, he moved on. Two days after his final game, Payton and Suhey went hunting in the marshes of northwestern Illinois. "A friend of ours had a big farm, and we went up there to hunt," Matt recalls. "Our friends Nick and Paul went, too, dragging through the snow. We shot a lot of pheasant and grouse. Walter was a great shot."

After that, Matt and Walter saw each other less, as they were no longer on the same schedule. They led very different lives—Payton became involved in various business ventures, while Suhey remained in the NFL.

"I kept in contact with him," Matt remembers. "But I was raising my kids and getting up at five thirty in the morning to go to work. I didn't see him as much. So there was a period in there where I wasn't as social with him."

But in 1998, Walter's inner circle would be drawn together again. When Walter's health began to deteriorate, he would rely on his friends and family more than ever before. And Suhey was there.

Suhey realized something was wrong when he saw Payton at an Indy car race in Detroit. "He had lost about thirty pounds," Suhey explains. "He had been in Panama with Mike Lanigan, who was Walter's partner in Payton Power Equipment, and I thought maybe he had caught a bug or some intestinal flu. I was joking around with him about losing weight."

After four months, when Payton hadn't gained the weight back, Suhey began to press for answers. But the ever-private Payton would not admit that anything was wrong.

"He had a great deal of pride," Suhey says. "And he needed to work through all this stuff himself. I think maybe he had his blinders on as to what was really wrong." But Suhey wouldn't let his friend shrug him off.

"He finally told me he was really sick," Suhey recalls. "He got real angry about it. And a few days later, he was going to the Mayo clinic for tests. To be honest with you, I really forced myself on him. Because he wasn't giving me any answers." It didn't matter that the two friends had fallen out of touch over the past few years; Matt took up his old support position as if they were still on the field together.

Matt went with Walter to his appointment at the Mayo clinic. The silent communication the men had always enjoyed during games made it easier for Walter to deal with his sickness—with Matt, he didn't have to talk about his sickness.

"When he went there the first time, I sat outside the room," Matt remembers. "When Walter came out, I asked him, 'What did the doctor say?' and Walter didn't answer. That same day he had another meeting with them. And he says to me, 'Come on in.' I was in on the rest of the conversations at that point."

From that point forward, Matt played an active role in Walter's hospital visits. He would constantly question doctors about diagnosis, treatment and prognosis. "I wanted to know what was going on," he says. "'What does he have? And how are you going to treat it?'" Naturally, Walter never asked Matt to take any responsibility in his treatment. Matt just did it. "I think I just, quite frankly, assumed that I was going to do that," he says in a typically selfless manner.

Walter Payton had been diagnosed with bile duct cancer. And doctors knew by the time he came in for treatment that he had no chance for a full recovery.

As trusted partners and friends turned away from Walter, he came to rely on Suhey more and more. Despite Walter's quiet demeanor, especially when it came to personal issues, Matt knew that Walter appreciated his presence. "I think that he did, but it was part of the job," Matt says. More than anything, Matt was there to talk about whatever Walter felt like talking about. "Toward the end, we had some pretty good talks about Mississippi and about the time he spent around here."

But Walter kept up his good spirits to the end. Matt says, "I don't know if he ever fully accepted that he was going to die." Walter once commented

that his relationship with Matt was like a reverse of the famous friendship between Bears' legend Gale Sayers and teammate Brian Piccolo. When the white Piccolo died of cancer in 1969, Sayers was by his side. Their story inspired the movie *Brian's Song*. "But in that one, the white guy gets sick and dies," Walter once stated. "I said I wondered how come I couldn't be in that movie."

Walter, who was—in Matt's words—"addicted to the phone," would call his friend late at night. Once, toward the end, he called Matt at three in the morning. "Come take a ride with me," Matt remembers Walter asking. They ended up driving around town for hours. Neither said anything. And they didn't have to. Walter's days were numbered.

"The last time I saw him, we all knew it was a matter of hours," Matt says. "That was at his home. He had things that needed to be done for his privacy, so there was no press camped out on the lawn. The irony is that I took some heat for being private about it, but he wanted to preserve his dignity with pride." As usual, Matt knew what to do for Walter without being asked.

On November 1, 1999, Walter Payton died in his home.

Matt remains tight-lipped about those last days in Payton's home. "In so many words, he did tell me he knew I was trying to preserve his dignity. Connie felt the same way, too. She took great care of him. Not an easy thing. It was a difficult time for her and for the family." He is clearly still pained by the loss of his best friend. "Time might not heal all wounds," he says, "but time allows you to move forward."

Matt is still close with the Paytons and serves as the executor of Walter's estate. He is the trustee of Jarrett's and Brittney's funds.

Today, Suhey still guards Walter. Suhey cares more about his relationship with Walter Payton than his own fame. And because of this unique

friendship, Suhey is able to preserve the true persona, values and dedication of the American icon, Sweetness.

CHAPTER

09 | Life With Walter

by Connie Payton

- 1976, Chicago -

During Walter's first year with the Bears I was a senior at JSU. Once in a while, I would get to travel to Chicago with his mom, Alyne, to visit him. Before his rookie season, she had moved to Chicago to keep him from getting too lonely during training camp. Then during the regular season she would make extended visits, when Walter wasn't on the road, to cook and do what she could to soothe his spirits during perhaps the hardest year of his professional career.

He wasn't having the best games, and that was extremely hard for him to handle. It wasn't that the game of football was suddenly strange to Walter, it was the baggage that came with playing as a professional that was all so new. That was an adjustment in his life that I don't think he planned on. And I think it made him feel lonely. This loneliness was apparent at the end of each visit, when Walter would beg me to stay with him. But I wouldn't budge. I knew I had to go back for school and that I couldn't stay with him. Plus, in those days that type of unmarried, courting lifestyle just wasn't done. Had I stayed, not only would his mother have been upset, but

my mother would have killed me! Needless to say, I stayed in Jackson for his first year in Chicago.

After his rookie season, Walter returned home to Mississippi. When the time came for him to return to Chicago for training camp for the summer, his mood changed and he became noticeably quiet. You could tell he was anticipating the worst part of playing in Chicago: feeling lonesome. I knew he wanted me to go to Chicago with him, so I gave him somewhat of an ultimatum.

I told him, "If you want me to be there with you, then we need to be together the right way." Walter knew only too well what I meant by this, so I didn't have to go into detail.

He never ceased to amaze me, least of all with his response to my ultimatum. He said, "So let me get this straight. If I don't marry you, you really aren't going to come to Chicago?" To which I promptly replied, "Noooo, I am really not going. I'm not going to do it." Oddly enough, I knew at that point that I wanted to spend the rest of my life with him, and with that smirk on his face when he challenged me, I knew that he wanted the same thing. And so he married me.

He used to tease me all the time that I made him do it. The day he came home with the ring, he told me he would make all the wedding arrangements, that he would do it all. He talked with Reverend Cameron, one of the pastors at Mount Cathray Baptist Church. This was one of the churches the kids on campus attended. He called two of his friends to be our witnesses; of course, they were friends from the football team.

The day we were to be married, I'm embarrassed to say, I forgot all about it! Walter had arranged for us to be in the pastor's chambers to take our vows, but I was out at the mall wandering around with some friends. I came home that evening with shopping bags, only to find him sitting in my

living room, pouting. He looked at me and said, "We were supposed to be in Reverend Cameron's chambers an hour ago." Needless to say, I think he was a little upset! He continued with a heated line of questioning, "How dare you forget this day? First you're going to make me marry you, and then you forget the day!" But when my mind is made up, it's made up, so I said, "I'm ready to go! Let's go now!"

Neither of our families was at our wedding, because we didn't tell them what we had planned. I mean, what Walter planned. Obviously, my mother was not happy with me when she found out what we had done. She was especially disappointed about how I had done it, because I am the oldest and the only girl in the family. I felt horrible for disappointing her, but I knew in my heart that I should marry Walter. Later I told her, "Mom, you and Daddy work so hard every day, and to even give me the wedding you would feel I wanted would have been a financial burden. I don't want you to feel like this is something you have to do for me." But God bless those people who really want a big, fancy wedding. I know with Brittney it will be a big ordeal. I also know that Walter wouldn't have it any other way.

All was not lost, though, or forgotten. For our tenth anniversary, Walter surprised me with a beautiful and proper wedding. He had the same minister, the same two witnesses—everyone. He brought them all back! We had the wedding we never had at home. My father walked me down the aisle, and I happened to wear white to dinner that night, so it was absolutely perfect. I couldn't stop smiling. It was such a wonderful day. And it only confirmed what I already knew: that ten years earlier Walter had

A young Jarrett pulling on his Auntie Pam's sweater with Walter's mother, Alyne and I outside of Soldier Field

made me the happiest woman in the world. At that moment, with my family around me, I felt so incredibly happy and blessed.

- 1984, Breaking Jim Brown's Rushing Record -

As a dutiful wife and, more importantly, a huge fan, I went to all the home games. I didn't travel to every away game, because it was easier to watch them on TV. It captured more of what was going on out in the field, and I didn't miss a play. I enjoyed attending all of the home games; in fact, I looked forward to them. For me, watching Walter on the field was no different from being in the shoes of any other fan. I was always in awe of how he played; he was a joy to watch. I was so proud of him and the talent he brought to "his" team. He truly loved playing with the Chicago Bears.

When the kids were really young, I rarely brought them to the games. Today, things are so much easier for the players' families. They have a comfortable area for them to sit inside and other accommodations. I recently told Jarrett, his teammates and their wives that they don't know how easy they have it with private boxes with heating. Soldier Field would get so cold. I didn't want our kids to freeze out there! But, whether it was twenty below or one hundred and twenty degrees outside, I knew *I* was going.

One of the most memorable times in Walter's career came after he had been playing for a number of years and had become better known. The time was so exciting for all of us. It was the game that hinged on him breaking Jim Brown's rushing record. His mom even came up from Mississippi with his sister Pam. At that time Jarrett was a little boy, but I brought him to the game, too. It was important for all of us to be there, especially because it was so important to Walter. After the game, there was a lot of celebrating and media attention. The fans were so elated, and that made Walter even happier. Afterwards, we all went home together for dinner. Walter's mom loved to cook for her youngest son. Anything he wanted, he could have. She prepared a wonderful dinner that we all enjoyed, and we talked and celebrated together at home. It was always special to be with family and just be home.

Throughout the years, Walter's playing brought so many people together.

It united fans across the nation who cheered him on. It unified his team, that group of men who work as a unit toward a common goal. Most importantly, though, it brought together a family by giving them something they could all watch and participate in, in whatever way they could.

- Retirement -

When Walter retired from football, the void in his life that he knew would be there hit him hard. He just wasn't the type of guy who could enjoy what "retirement" has to offer. To the majority of people it is a time

to relax and take one day at a time. This new lifestyle was not for Walter. Instead, he had to ask himself, "What am I going to do now? What do I do with myself?"

That's when he started racing cars. He needed something to fill the hours that football had once dominated. He was hesitant to accept all that downtime. He had played football all of his life, which for him created a structured routine—practice, play a game on Sunday, train on Tuesday, travel Wednesday. I don't think retirement is an easy time for any athlete. These

guys are conditioned to play football, basketball or whatever every single day of their lives. It doesn't matter where they are or how well off they are financially—it is a struggle for them to leave it all behind. They need to readjust. But honestly, I didn't get it. I thought after all of those years of running, playing and practicing that Walter would be physically, emotionally and mentally ready to just rest his body and relax a little. But it's not that simple. It's truly not that simple to let it go.

Walter's new interest eased the transition. Driving fueled his adrenaline addiction. The thrill of speeding the car around the track gave him a rush similar to that of being on the field, and he loved it. Practice and preparation also took up a lot of his time, returning structure and routine to his life. It gave him an outlet for all the discipline that he had gained from his years of training.

While Walter embraced this new passion of his later life, his football glory days were never to be forgotten.

- Football Hall of Fame -

Walter had been retired for five years when he was nominated to the Hall of Fame. It was a tremendous honor for us, so we were looking forward to going to Canton, Ohio. Walter had a tough time deciding who he would

let induct him, only because there were so many people that were important to him. Everyone was eager to know, who was going to do the honors? When he chose Jarrett, who was twelve years old that year, he ended the controversy. What could anyone say, right? It was the perfect choice.

Jarrett was initially nerve-wracked about the speech. But after he got over the fact that he couldn't wear his tennis shoes and realized what an honor it was, he was okay with it. It was great for him. He was able to be with his dad, go shopping and attend all the dinners and the parades. Once we got there, you couldn't even tell that he was nervous. I think I was more anxious than anybody, wondering how he was going to get up in front of all those people and deliver his speech. As it turned out, I needn't have worried. He was wonderful. Walter and I were so proud of him.

- The Foundation -

Even after enjoying the benefits reaped from his life on the field, Walter never forgot his humble beginnings. He liked to contribute in ways that made a difference that people recognized and appreciated, but didn't know were from him. He was more concerned about the power and usefulness of his gestures than about getting credit. His generosity toward others truly came from his heart.

This was one of the reasons he felt so at home with the Bears. Many of his teammates' hearts were in the same place. They were very driven to get involved with their communities and spread kindness to people less fortunate—letting the underprivileged know that they are not forgotten. To let them know that people do care and are watching out for them.

Walter always reserved a soft spot in his heart for children. He studied special education while he played football at Jackson State, and for part of his degree, he was a student teacher. He truly loved going out and working with these kids, getting them to respond to him in ways that other people couldn't. It delighted him. You could tell from the pitch in his voice and the look in his eyes that this was his passion, that he unequivocally loved these kids. I think if he hadn't played football, he would have made a tremendous difference in this respect. He would have made an excellent teacher and been a wonderful influence in the lives of special-needs kids. Teaching is the ultimate form of giving, and for that he had a real talent.

Walter felt a strong need to do something for kids who were growing up with little or next to nothing. His opportunity came in 1985, shortly

before his retirement. He was on top of the world careerwise, so he was able to use his name in setting up a foundation dedicated to improving the lives of neglected and underprivileged children in the Chicago area. He named it the George Halas/Walter Payton Foundation. Typical Walter—he put his idol first. Establishing the Foundation was the realization of one of his biggest dreams. It made his work on the football field more than a game. The game became real—he was helping others, and it inspired him.

He tried to reach out to people on a daily basis. For example, Jeanie Ortega-Piron, a DCFS worker who went to the Payton Foundation to ask for a donation, always tells a story about arriving at the Foundation's offices in the spring of 1997. "I looked at a sign to determine which way to turn," she remembers, "when suddenly I felt these very big arms around me. There he was, Walter Payton himself. And what he said amazed me. He was asking me if I had gotten lost coming to the office, that he had been waiting and that he hoped I'd choose them to help the children. Choose them? I was there to ask him for money. What was he talking about?"

That, too, was typical Walter: he saw the opportunity to help others as a privilege he was lucky to have.

Walter's life, too, was changing, though in ways far less beneficial.

It's strange, really, when I think about how we became aware that something was wrong with Walter. There were signs, but we didn't pay enough attention to them.

- Sickness -

When Walter began racing, he had to take a number of physicals. Several doctors noted that he had high enzyme counts in his liver but never really went in depth and questioned it.

I don't blame Walter for not being more fastidious about being thoroughly checked up. He dealt with the discomfort like he famously had on the field—by sucking it up. I remember that if he would eat certain things, he would have severe stomach cramps. He practically lived on Maalox and Pepto-Bismol to calm his stomach down. It would hurt for a while, but then it would be gone and he'd be back to normal again.

Eight years later, he could no longer deny that something was wrong. Doctors confirmed that his stomach cramps and his high enzyme count were symptomatic of advanced liver disease known as primary sclerosing cholangitis (PSC). Frustratingly, the only thing we could do to help him was help him keep a healthier diet and be more diligent about taking certain vitamins. We knew it wouldn't reverse the condition, but it might slow it down while we waited for that only hope—a liver transplant.

I think that somehow, because everybody knows their own body, Walter had to have known that something was going on long before the liver disease diagnosis. But the doctors and people surrounding him just kind of shrugged it off to being hit so many times. And so did he.

I talked to someone else about Walter's reaction, and they said it's a male thing. Men never want to admit that they are sick. My father is a prime example; he ignored a knot on his neck for some time. My mother was aware of this and encouraged him to have it checked, but my dad continued to say, "Oh, it's all right." Finally, my mother made him go to the doctor, only to find he had stage-four lymphoma. If it had been up to him, he would've never gone to the doctor. I don't know if it's denial or fear or

what. What I do know is that when Walter got hurt on the field, he pushed through it. He never wanted to let his team or his fans down. In this case, our family was his team, and he was determined to shake it off and keep playing. He didn't want to believe he was hurt, because he didn't want to hurt or disappoint us.

In an effort to finally put gossip to rest about his health issues, Walter held a press conference on February 2, 1999, and shared with the world his need for a liver transplant.

After this press conference aired, Walter in his infamous way continued to help others by pairing with Jesse White on TV in a commercial that promoted the awareness of the need for organ donors. This short clip was instrumental in the state of Illinois turning out record numbers of registered donors, which resulted in Illinois jumping to number one in the U.S. for number of registered donors. We remain number one to this day. The state of Illinois initiated a commemorative organ donor license plate in remembrance of the man who never tired of extending help to others.

Unfortunately, weeks after this press conference was held, Walter was diagnosed with cancer of the bile duct, a vessel that carries digestive fluids from the liver to the small intestine. The exploratory surgery on May 10, 1999, revealed that the cancer had spread into his lymph nodes, which was devastating news and certainly not the news Walter had wanted to hear. The malignancy was very advanced and progressed very rapidly. Now that he had cancer, he was ineligible for a transplant, yet without the new liver, he really didn't have the strength to go through treatment to fight the cancer. Had he not developed cancer, I know in my heart of hearts he would have been the recipient of the transplant he needed and everything would have been fine. But that was not his fate.

I think it was hard for the kids to see their dad getting sicker and more frail, but Walter was always smiling and staying positive. He was trying to be there for the kids, and he always wanted them to know that their dad was there for them. Walter didn't want them to see him sick, because he knew in their eyes he was their Superman. Walter's health was definitely taking a turn for the worse. He could no longer hide the inevitable.

When he was ill and sleeping a lot, Walter spent time in each of the kids' rooms. He moved himself into Jarrett's room for a while, and shortly thereafter, he moved into Brittney's room.

The morning he passed, Walter was in our bedroom. For the months beforehand, we hadn't given much thought to the time he had been spending in the kids' rooms. But after he passed away, we were happy he had made such a conscious effort. I don't know if he purposely spent time in their rooms to stay connected with them or if he just felt in his heart that he should be there. But after he died, Brittney and Jarrett said that they could feel his comforting presence in their rooms. Now we understand what he was trying to do, and apparently it worked.

We continue to feel Walter's presence in so many ways, but especially through the memories we have of him. These are the things that we hold on to. When I look at the picture from the night of Brittney's eighth-grade dance, there is a sweetness and a sadness to it. You can see how proud of her he looks and how happy she is to have him there. I think that picture is the last one of Walter and Brittney together. It's a special picture for us because it reminds us of a happy time when we were all together as a family. Jarrett was graduating from high school that year, and we had a graduation party with family and friends. It was really nice that Walter was able to celebrate this joyful time with all of us.

- Faith -

As a family, we never questioned our faith. We knew better, because our faith has been a constant strength and vital part of all of our lives. We were always surrounded by people with such strong convictions. Their prayers and uplifting words meant so much to us during hard times.

We knew we were in for a battle once we understood the extent of Walter's illness. Without our faith, we would have never had the courage to face each new day. We needed to believe that no matter what happened, we would be strong enough to see it through. Everything that was happening was a part of destiny: our destiny as a family and Walter's personal destiny. We weren't going to question it; instead we prayed for continued strength to accept it. We were always spiritual and had faith in God, but the Lord never played as large a role in our lives as He did at that time.

Once he was diagnosed with cancer, we were definitely scared. When we knew there was nothing we could do to reverse his condition, all we could do was stay faithful and positive. Spiritual life was something we relied on a lot in those days. We went to church and prayed together, and it was a relief to have a source of strength when Walter was losing his.

Our faith continues to be a large part of our lives. I think the kids are thankful that they were raised in the church and can tap into that spirituality. They are on their own now, but I'm not worried about them. They have that pillar to rely on through all of their tough times, as well as their triumphs.

People ask how we could remain optimistic in the face of such trying circumstances. My answer? Faith. I know that some things are out of my control, and I believe in something higher and more powerful then me. Whatever happens, we're going to be okay through it all. That makes a big difference.

- The Final Game -

Less than a week after Walter passed, the children and I found ourselves at Soldier Field in Chicago for a memorial tribute celebrating the life of a man who had become one of the city's own. Chicago loved Walter, and he loved Chicago. During that time on the field, everyone sensed that he wasn't far away. The tribute was so touching that at times it saddened me. Deep down I knew I had to be strong for the sake of Jarrett and Brittney. That strength was passed on from the love I felt from those wonderful people attending the service, and it was amazing. That's when I knew, my God, this man was truly blessed beyond what he could have ever imagined.

In the period immediately following Walter's service, there was one incident that reminded me how far his popularity reached and how universal his appeal was. I was going to Jackson on a plane for something, and during a layover in Atlanta, the lady sitting next to me told me that her whole family had flown back home to Chicago to have a service for Walter at their house. She said that when they watched the memorial service on TV everyone was completely silent. She recalled, "You would have thought

Bobby Engram and Marty Booker observe a moment of silence at a pre-game tribute to Walter at Lambeau Field before the November 7, 1999 Bears-Packers Game.

we had lost one of our own family members, the way we were carrying on." I have to say, for me, that was one of those "wow" moments.

Incidents such as these helped me mourn and eventually begin to heal. I re-committed myself to the kind of work Walter had begun with the foundation. The opportunity to throw myself into the foundation, and not think about me but about the kids and what they needed, was my therapy and helped with my grieving process. I thought about how Walter would be so proud that we'd still continue the foundation in his name. It was

Bobby Engram pulls in the go ahead touchdown past the Packers' Antuan Edwards.

Bryan Robinson blocks a 27-yeard field goal attempt by Green Bay's Ryan Longwell to secure a Bear win.

really a good way for me to work myself through the entire experience of dealing with something that I couldn't believe had happened.

When my children and I look back on our last year with Walter, it wasn't just the support of family and friends that helped us get through the difficult times. We attribute a lot of that support to Walter's fans. For us, it's those fans that always believed in Walter, those who took the time to say a thank you when we needed it most. It's these special moments that we've held, and will continue to hold, dearest to our hearts.

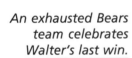

An exhausted Bears team celebrates Walter's last win.

In Walter's heart, he expressed through his book *Never Die Easy* not just his love for his fans and for football, but also the love and admiration he held for his children. He declared his feelings for his family with these words: "Jarrett and Brittney, football will not be my legacy. The two of you will. I love you both more than you'll ever know, probably more than I ever showed. I could not be more proud of where you two are headed. Keep straight and keep moving. And remember to tell your mother you love her."

Through it all, Walter was so on track with his thoughts. I'm no different than Walter in believing that our children are our greatest legacy, like any loving and struggling parent. I say that because it's true for all of us, it's not an easy task raising children, and more than anything I want Jarrett and Brittney to carry with them everything good that their father and I have taught them. That's what life is all about, as we all pass a torch to continue a circle of caring passed from generation to generation. Caring about each other is what life is all about and what was such an integral part of their father's life.

CHAPTER 10 | If You Want Me, Just Whistle

By Jarrett Payton

- Growing Up -

When I was growing up, I could always count on my dad to have my back no matter where I went or what I did. From my first games in high school he'd been a constant presence, always up there in the stands. And whenever he wanted to let me know he was there watching out for me, he'd just whistle. I'd turn my head, and there he'd be. That whistle became our special bond, almost like a secret handshake that only he and I knew about.

That whistle helped me get through a lot of tough times in my life. And even after my dad got sick, when he was facing the toughest battle of *his* life, I knew I could still count on that whistle to help me find some inner strength. I remember a

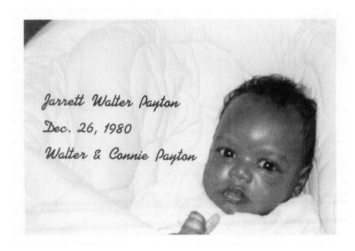

Jarrett Walter Payton
Dec. 26, 1980
Walter & Connie Payton

game I was playing up at Boston College while I was still a Miami Hurricane. This may seem like the strangest thing, but I was just standing on the sidelines, in between plays, and I swear I heard that whistle. It was so clear to me that I had to turn around. The funny thing is that I was so sure I had heard him I even started to look for him up in the stands, even though I knew he had to be at home watching the game on TV. This was only a few months before he passed away. Thinking about that game and that whistle lets me know that he's still watching my back, even today.

When I was growing up, I knew that my dad was something special. Not because he was the biggest running back, or the fastest, or the strongest, because he wasn't any of those things to me. Not by a long shot. But in my eyes, even as a little kid (and not just because he was my dad), I knew he was the smartest.

From the get-go, Dad knew that getting anywhere in the game wasn't about how much muscle you have but about how much willpower, or what the Payton family calls "want-to," you have. And my dad had more want-to than just about anybody in the league. He worked harder than anyone else, and that was the secret to his success, or at least part of it.

I'd say the other part of how he got so far was the way that he grew to really embrace his team as his family. They were his family in the sense that these were people who counted on him to give everything of himself, all the time, on every play, and not let them down. He knew that if he did that for them, they'd do the same for him in return. He never had to talk or say anything, since he wasn't much of a talker anyway. He let his actions do the talking, and anyone who saw how much heart and effort he put into his game would pretty much have no choice but to feel inspired to do the same.

My dad also taught me the importance of being flexible as a football player. Sure, it's great to excel at the running game, but the real value you bring to a team is being a complete player at any position on the field. Some of my favorite memories are of watching those plays when they'd hand the ball to my dad and he'd fake everybody out by turning into a quarterback and lobbing the ball downfield for a completion. I even remember a time when he lined up to kick a field goal!

People always ask me what it was like growing up as the son of a superstar. After all, back in the eighties he was to Chicago what Michael Jordan was to that city in the nineties. But despite all the fame, I always loved my dad for being so down to earth, for knowing that at the end of the day, it was the love he shared with me, my mom and my sister that mattered most.

I remember being chosen as the one to introduce my dad when he was inducted into the Hall of Fame in Canton, Ohio, in 1993. The funny thing is

"Payton's Hill"

In January 2000, the Arlington Heights Park District named this area "Payton's Hill" in honor of Walter Payton, running back for the Chicago Bears from 1975-1987. An eight-year resident of Arlington Heights, Walter used the hill for strength and endurance training while a member of the Chicago Bears.

Walter Payton's Records Include:
• 28 Chicago Bear and 7 NFL records
• 10 seasons with 1,000 or more yards rushing
• Single-game NFL rushing record of 275 yds.

Walter passed away on November 1, 1999 at the age of 45.

that with all the hype going on, he seemed most concerned with just making sure I was doing all right with the speech I was preparing. He asked me, "Are you okay?" and I always just said, "Yes," even though I was pretty nervous. In the speech, I called him my role model and my best friend. That's still true today.

Even when he broke Jim Brown's record, he still made sure that I never felt left out. The one memory I have of that crazy time is being with him in the stadium parking lot when he was presented with a Lamborghini to commemorate that amazing day. There were cameramen and reporters all trying to ask my dad questions. But he managed to get through all of them, and he picked me up in his arms. We got in the car and just sat inside and talked. It's like he just shut out all of the madness and took time out to chill with me in the front seat. I was just excited about the fact that I got to be inside the same car as the one in *Back to the Future*, with those cool doors that opened sideways. And of course, when we took it out for a spin, it was

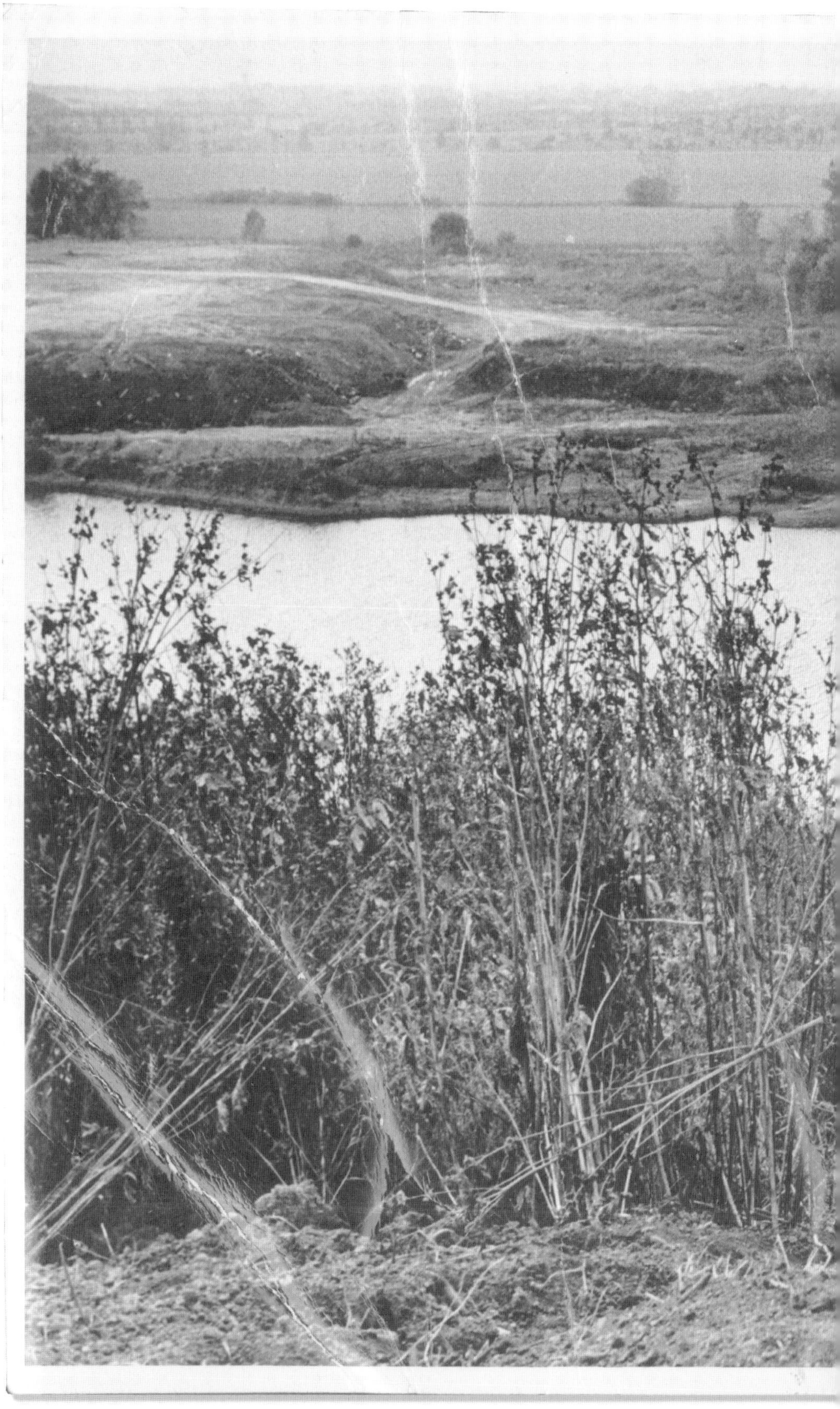

a fun ride. But like a lot of the glitzy things that came his way, it never really mattered that much to him. The car (and the gas mileage) wasn't him, so he gave it up pretty quickly.

His priorities just weren't about the showy stuff, either on or off the field. Besides looking after his family, which was always number one for him, his quest to always push himself to the limit and to surpass what anybody expected of him was his personal motivation.

That explains why his workouts were so legendary. Everyone seems to know about the Hill. I remember going to the Hill in Arlington Heights, Illinois, when I was little and watching him work out. He'd work out so hard that he couldn't even drive home. He was always joking with me, saying, "You wanna run?" And I saw how steep that hill was. There was no way at that age that I could have run it. I saw him take grown men out there, and they'd be talking about how they could run that hill any time. They'd run up that hill two times. Their legs would be gone. Half of them would go to the hospital. It really was a test of a person's willpower.

- Coming Into My Own -

In some ways, being the son of Walter Payton has its own difficulties. Particularly because of who he was, there are always going to be comparisons and certain expectations. But I knew, right from the start, that I needed to step out of his shadow. I needed to make it on my own and to be recognized in my own right.

The great thing about having Walter Payton as a dad was that, despite how much he achieved, he *never* pressured me to "do this" or "do that." The funny thing is that when I first became interested in sports, football wasn't really my passion. The first sport I ever played was soccer. He didn't understand it at first. And here's the great thing about my dad: even with his busy schedule, he still put the time in to learn as much as he could about the game, and he quickly became a fan. Toward the end of my first two high school years, he was there at every game—right by the goalpost.

Of course, it was just a matter of time before my love for football developed. And I think my dad knew in his heart that it was always going to happen. As much as I was already getting compared to him in soccer, it was ten times worse in football. I remember when I told Coach Kelly at school, who was a friend of my dad's, about wanting to tackle football. News traveled fast. When I got home, my dad called. He said, "You know it's gonna be hard, right?" And I said, "Yeah, I know." And he said, "All right, I just wanted to tell you." He never said I couldn't do it. He just loved everything I did.

I know a lot of what he was trying to instill in me has helped me tremendously. Once I started college at the University of Miami, I think he knew he wasn't going to be around for a long time. He did things I didn't understand then—like teaching me about hard work. He made me work at Payton Power Equipment over the summer—I had to be there all day and work from the bottom up. If he hadn't done that, I wouldn't be the strong person I am today. He was putting me in those difficult situations then so I could handle them on my own now.

Even right now, as I'm playing in NFL Europe, I'm realizing that the values he brought to his game can make all the difference in the world. After some games my shoulders hurt so much it's hard for me to sleep. But that's okay with me, because it just means I've really gotten into my dad's mindset about the game, where you leave everything out there on the playing field and worry about the aches and pains later.

Just like my dad felt at the beginning of his career, I have a whole team in Amsterdam backing me up, rooting for me to succeed. It's wonderful how this all came together in such a short period of time.

Now we're in contention for the World Bowl. That's how I always wanted it to be, how I envisioned things when I was younger. At crunch time, the guys look to me to get the job done. For instance, I had a touchdown run last night that turned out to be the spark that started everything. So you never know what the real impact of that one play, or that one extra yard, will be. That's the message of my dad's career.

And I love all these great Dutch fans that I've met during my time here as an Amsterdam Admiral. To be honest, it's crazy the way they treat me over here. It's really something else to see your name on a banner. When I see banners that say "SWEETNESS ALL OVER AGAIN," or I read that people here have nicknamed me "Baby Sweetness" and "Nutra Sweet," it's hard not to be moved. But perhaps the most emotional part of this whole experience is when my mom sees me play. In the beginning, she was always nervous about the fact that I decided to play professionally.

She thought it was too rough. But then, after she watched me play, she told me she saw Dad in me. That was probably the biggest compliment I've received during my time playing ball.

I know my dad was one of a kind and that there will never be another Sweetness, but as he himself would be the first to tell you, that shouldn't stop you from trying to climb that hill.

CHAPTER

11 | In His Shadow

By Brittany Payton

- Losing My Dad -

Losing my dad was something that took me a long time to begin to heal from. To the outside world, he was a lot of different things: Sweetness, the heart of the Chicago Bears, perhaps even the greatest running back in league history. As a philanthropist, he changed countless lives through his foundation. But to me, he was just my dad, the man who raised me, who was always there for me when I needed a helping hand, a shoulder to cry on or someone to talk to. People say that he was taken too young from the world at age forty-five. All I know is that at age fourteen, I felt like a part of me had been lost forever. It's been almost six years since my dad passed away, and the grief and loss still hurt so much.

But the story of how I learned to get back on my feet owes a lot to my dad (as well as my mom). In the end, I almost think it is *his* strength that helps carry me through difficult times.

After he died, I started to withdraw from everything and everyone around me. In retrospect, I think this was just a natural way for me to try to deal with the pain. I remember hating the feeling I had when teachers at school started pulling me aside the week after my dad's death, telling me how sorry they were and asking me if I needed anything. Looking back, I know now that they meant well, but at the time I resented it because it singled me out in front of everyone else. And lots of times when they'd come up, I'd just start crying, because I just wished they'd leave me alone.

Losing a parent is always hard. But when that parent happens to be someone who was in the public spotlight and was a larger-than-life hero to so many, it becomes even harder. You're walking through the halls at school, and everyone is staring at you because you've had the six o'clock news flooding your lawn that day to report to the world that your dad passed away.

The truth is that my dad's fame has always been a mixed blessing for me. It's hard to explain to those who haven't been through it, but when you're a kid, the pressure can almost be too intense. Sometimes it made me wish I was more like a normal teenager, with a dad who had a nine-to-five job—not a dad whose every move was watched by millions, on and off the field. I wanted him just for me, us, our family.

A lot of people's favorite memories of my dad may be this touchdown, or that run, or perhaps the games during the Super Bowl season, but I was too young to really remember all of that. When I think of my favorite memories of my dad, it always comes back to the little things that we did together as father and daughter. When I was a kid, my dad took me to the Mall Of America in Minneapolis/St. Paul, which is the largest shopping mall in the entire country. It was basically just a little father-daughter trip for the two of us. Even as a child, I felt the excitement of my dad's knack for shopping as we explored the huge mall and picked out gifts together.

Even today, it brings a smile to my face to remember how on this trip, my dad, this super athlete who had done pretty much everything a man could on the playing field, had so much trouble trying to do something as simple

as braiding my hair. I kept turning around, telling him how to do it right. I can still picture my dad whenever I braid my hair. Remembering how he took the time to learn how to do it right still brings a smile to my face.

Another fond memory I have of my father is him putting me in the car on the nights when I couldn't sleep. He would put on WNUA, one of the local radio stations, and we would just listen to jazz music until I fell asleep. It was such a simple thing to do, but it meant a lot to me to know that he was always thinking about me and how I was doing.

I think my dad knew that Jarrett and I were not comfortable with all the media attention that surrounded him. We could tell he tried to shield us from all the publicity as best he could. For example, when we weren't around he was always such an incredibly giving and generous person when it came to speaking with his fans, signing autographs and everything else that made him special to those who wanted to meet him. But when we *were* around, Dad had a tendency to hold back a bit. Even as kids, Jarrett and I both sensed that maybe this was his way of protecting us from a limelight that we were still too young to understand.

- Trying to Regain Control -

Ultimately, facing the death of someone you love really makes you realize how little control you have when it comes to the game of life; you'd be surprised how hard we try to deny this basic truth about our lives. I know I did. I pretended I had control when I didn't. In my case, food became one arena in which I would try to exert my control. Right after my father's death, I started to eat less and less. Of course, everyone who knew me noticed that something was going on, but I was oblivious to all this. I had no idea I had begun to develop an eating disorder. Even though I was losing a lot of weight, it was hard for me to realize that through not eating I was losing control over my body, not gaining it.

It was only after I started seeing a therapist that I started to see the elaborate way in which I was playing out these control issues. Withdrawing,

not eating, all of this was a way to avoid the sense of pain that hit me after my dad died.

I felt I was on track, but I suffered a setback when I came down with mononucleosis – not life threatening by any means, but the doctors needed to clear me with a clean bill of health so I could return to school. It was at this time that my doctor thought he saw something suspicious and ordered a full CAT scan. What they discovered was a growth on my pancreas. Without even waiting, they operated and removed it. Everyone, including all my family and friends, waited on pins and needles to see if it was benign or not. Luckily, it was, but because of my father, the possibility of cancer was always looming in the background.

After high-school graduation, and with my mom's blessing, I decided to attend the University of Arizona to pursue a career as a nurse-anesthesiologist. I truly felt that being away from home and venturing out on my own were things I needed to do to help me grow. But what I ultimately learned was that I wanted and needed to be home, surrounded by my family and Chicago, the city that continues to embrace the Paytons and that has become such a vital part of who we are.

When I arrived back home, one of the things I was most looking forward to was spending a lot of time hanging out with Nicole, my best friend since grade school. Like me, she had just returned home from her school. We talked a lot about the fun we'd soon be having in the city.

But only a few days later, she took her own life.

Once again, I was devastated. Nicole was like my sister. Growing up, the two of us had done everything together. She was the one who held my hand at my father's funeral. Her death took me by total surprise. Once again, I learned that I had no control, not even when it came to the people I loved most.

- Finding Peace -

But then a curious thing happened. It began one night with a dream.

After my dad passed, I had dreams about him for some time. So seeing him in my dreams wasn't out of the ordinary. For instance, I remember the first one that I had. He appeared in a spot in our old house. And he was telling me that he couldn't stay for long, but he'd be back again. And two days later, I had another dream. It was great, because of the way he looked— he was healthy again, and he was just so happy. He told me that it was okay and that he didn't want me to be upset. In these dreams, I could tell that he was trying to bring me peace.

And then, the day after Nicole passed, he came to me again. Yet again, I had a sense of him being there, comforting me simply with his presence, letting me know that he was watching over me and Nicole. It was after this dream that I really knew that everything was going to be okay.

It's hard to explain, but from that moment on, that night when he came to visit me in my sleep, I knew that I was slowly coming to terms with death in general. Not just *his* death. Not just Nicole's death. I was slowly learning to let go of trying to control my life and was starting to appreciate what each day can hold. My father always found a way to stay on his feet on the field, and now he was helping me to stay on mine. While he was alive, he was a firm believer that "tomorrow is promised to no one." That's why he played each game like it was his last. And even as a player, he knew there was so much he couldn't control, so why even worry about it? He just focused on what he could control, which was really nothing more than his will to never give up. That's what carried him past the goal line when others would have fallen short.

Of course, it took time to really internalize all of this. But slowly, that happened. One day, after months of not being able to see Nicole's grave site, I finally felt ready. My father was cremated, so I'd never been to a cemetery before. A lot of friends wanted to go with me, knowing how difficult it would be for me. In the end, I knew I had to face this alone, just as I had faced my dad's death. I brought two white roses to the cemetery and ended up sitting by the headstone for hours, talking to my friend. Even today, when I'm having a particularly rough time, I'll just go there and sit. It's very peaceful, and it keeps me connected.

I still wear a piece of my dad's Super Bowl ring around my neck. As a part of the Payton family, I know that football will always be associated with our name. But for me, my father is less about all the miraculous plays he made on the field than about those quiet moments we shared together while he was alive, and which he still shares with me in my dreams. It was in these precious moments that he taught me what really matters in life.

Now, when I find myself unable to sleep, I just think of my dad and get into my car (which I call Miss B because that's the nickname my dad gave me). With my dad in my heart, I turn the radio to WNUA, and together, we just go for a ride. This time I'm the one behind the wheel, but he's still there next to me. Together, we just drive along, taking the turns carefully, with as much speed as is safe. And like my dad, I'm taking on the world with my foot heavy on the gas and my eye on the future—knowing that it is promised to no one—and determined to live each day to the fullest.

AFTERWORD

My Father's Legacy

By Jarrett Payton

As I look back on just how much my dad meant to me, I keep thinking about my my freshman year at the University of Miami. The football program at UM is one of the most dominant in the country. That was something my dad and I had talked about a lot before I actually left for school. We spoke about how I was embarking on a new and exciting chapter in my life. One phase of my life was coming to a close, and another was about to begin. At the time, I didn't realize how this would be true in more ways than one.

Once I got there, I became part of the active roster. I'd like to think that the coaching staff was just so impressed by my moves that they instantly decided to throw me in there, but something tells me that there was more to it. In all honesty, it was a series of injuries on the team that allowed me to skip the typical freshman redshirt year. Arriving in Miami in August of '99, still uncertain of the outcome of my dad's health, I felt as if a higher power was somehow helping me face this difficult period by granting my dad the opportunity to see me suit up at the collegiate level.

I was called home by Mom as Dad worsened. What normally would be considered a short flight suddenly seemed endless. It gave me time to reflect on the strength of our family and the role I would be taking. Back home, I was able to spend some time with my father and be there to comfort Mom and Brittney. Upon my dad's passing, Mom wanted us to get back to our regular routines, and for me that was returning to school and football.

I have to admit that it was really hard to return to the football field knowing that my biggest advocate was no longer going to be in the stands. But I eventually came to realize that my dad was even closer—even within speaking distance. He was right where he has always been—in my heart. I was thrilled when, a few games after my return, I went in for a touchdown, and I immediately pointed to the sky. It was my way of giving credit to the man who guided me across the goal line and who had taught me so much about both life and football.

My dad's legacy isn't all that complicated: Be the very best you can be, and the rest will follow. Don't focus on what you can't control, but only on what you can. Just do your best by giving everything you've got and leaving it all out on the field.

Maybe that explains why my dad never put much stock in stats and records. He once said, "Records are just like dreams: good while you're having them, but then when you wake up, you can't remember them." He didn't particularly appreciate the media's insistence on comparing and ranking great running backs. To him, it was as pointless as "trying to draw the wind." After all, each individual player ought to be appreciated for his unique talent.

Coach Ditka, who coached my dad for his last six seasons, said that he was the best football player he had ever seen because he could do so many

things so well. My dad loved not just to run with the ball but to block for others. He knew how to catch, to throw and to return punts and kickoffs. He was even the Bears' backup kicker! And though I think he loved being a star running back, I'm sure he loved the feeling of just being one of the guys even more.

Because he really didn't see himself as that different from anybody else, he was always a bit surprised when people wrote him letters telling him how much he had meant to them. And because he was, above all else, a humanitarian, he truly appreciated and valued the impact he had on the lives of others. The fact that they took the time to tell him of the hope and joy that he had brought to them over the years really touched him.

After my father learned of the illness that would ultimately take his life, countless letters poured in to our home every day. "When I was able to look at the hundreds of thousands of lives that I've affected," he said, "I was blown away. Because, you know, you think, 'Well, I went out of my way to go and speak to this person, oh, I did this.' You'd think after all these years, they would have forgotten. I've gotten fan mail from people that I met fifteen years ago, and it still meant the same to them as the day I talked to them. I didn't realize—I really, for the first time, got it."

Actually, I think he always got it. You see, my dad once told me who he liked to play for whenever he took the field. For him, he had a special place in his heart for those fans who sat out in the nosebleed seats. He knew that these were die-hard fans who shelled out their hard-earned cash, and often came from great distances, just to see the team they loved. Maybe they could afford to come see the Bears play only once a year. Maybe it would be the only chance they got in their entire lifetime to see the Bears play.

Because he knew what they went through just to be there, he wanted to put on a great show for them, every time. It was as if he thought that might be their only chance to see him. He wanted to make that game shine for them. That's who he played for. And now that's who I play for.

Even as he loved to play for those fans in the nosebleeds, now I feel like he's my own nosebleed fan—sitting way up there, too far for the eye to see, watching me and waiting to see what comes next.

And if I happen to hear a whistle coming from way up in the stands, I won't need to look up. I'll already know who's there.

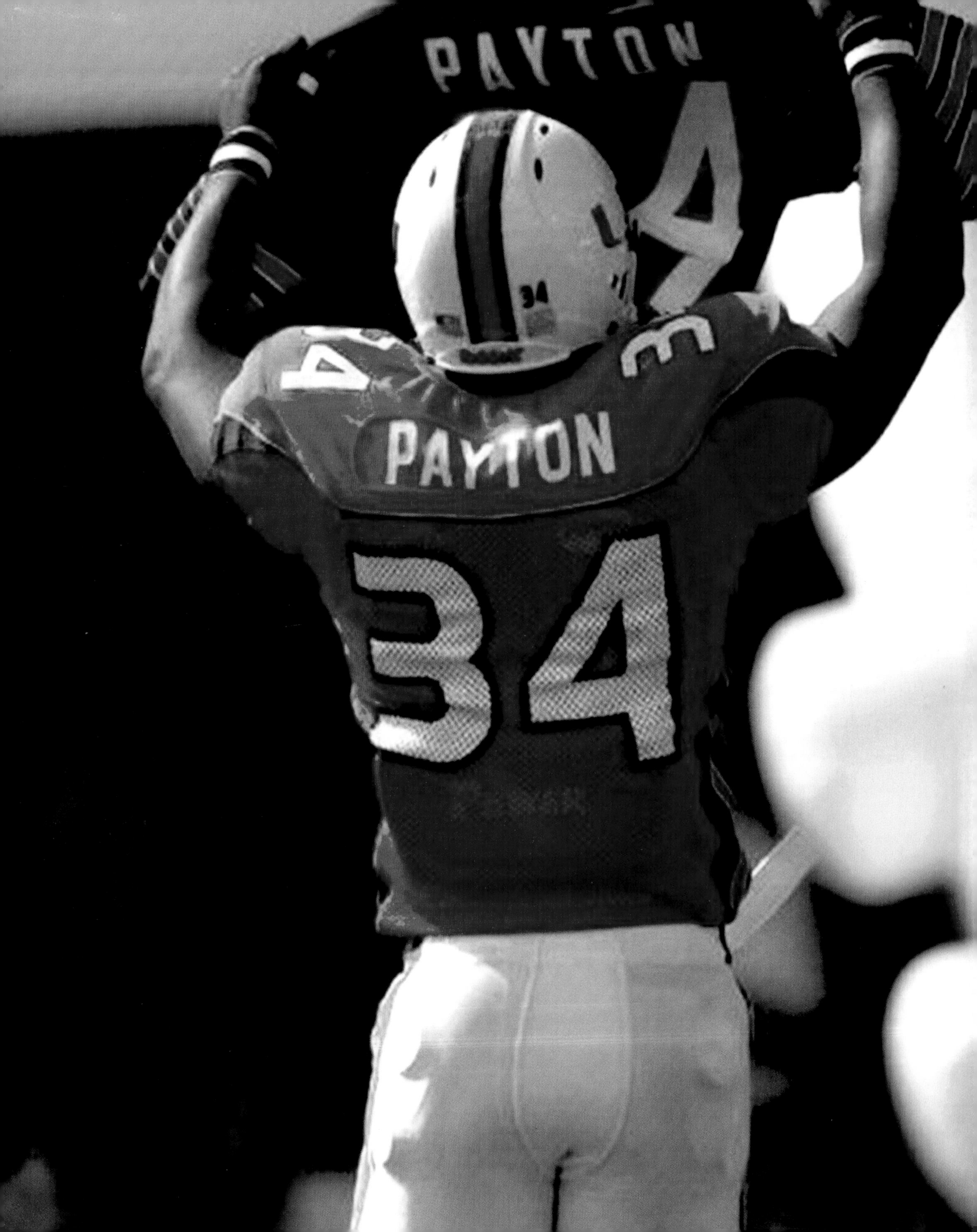

PAYTON
34
PAYTON
34

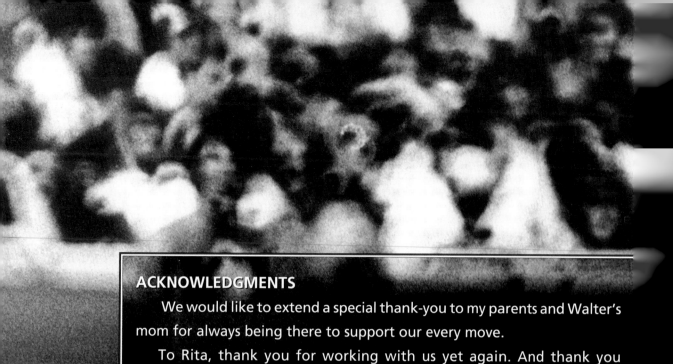

ACKNOWLEDGMENTS

We would like to extend a special thank-you to my parents and Walter's mom for always being there to support our every move.

To Rita, thank you for working with us yet again. And thank you especially to Kelly and Matt and the kids—I can't thank you enough for all your hard work and dedication to this book and our family. We are so very blessed to have close friends and family that continue to rally around us.

Thank you to Rugged Land Books and the people who worked so hard to help with this project: Alexa Bedell-Healy, Bruce Bennett, David Ling, Christian Moerk and Edward Smith. Many thanks to Roy Firestone and ESPN.

With this book we hoped to bring a personal insight into not just the professional life of running back Walter Payton, but his life as a husband, father and friend. Today the legacy he left behind still flourishes and, prayerfully, will forever.

My dearest Jarrett and Brittney, as your father said, you are his greatest legacy. I know in my heart that your dad shares the pride that I have for you today. May God continue to bless you. I love you both, Mom.

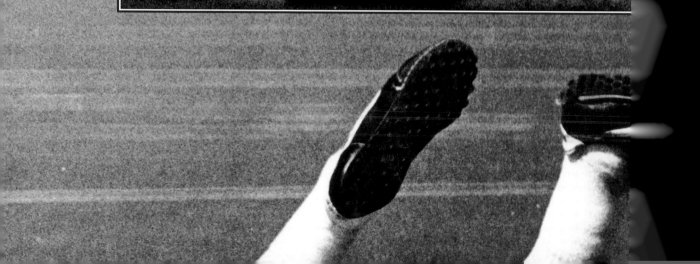

TOP 10 AVERAGE PER CARRY DAYS

1)	10.16	(18-183) vs. Saints	December 14, 1980
2)	8.95	(20-179) vs. Broncos	September 9, 1984
3)	8.91	(23-205) at Green Bay	October 30, 1977
4)	7.91	(23-182) vs. Vikings	September 9, 1979
5)	7.42	(19-141) at Minnesota	October 10, 1976
6)	7.36	(19-140) vs. Saints	October 2, 1976
7)	7.13	(22-157) at Denver	October 16, 1978
8)	7.04	(23-162) at San Francisco	October 29, 1979
9)	6.95	(23-160) vs. Lions	September 18, 1977
10)	6.95	(20-139) at Tampa Bay	November 9, 1986

OPPONENT	GAMES	RUSHES	YARDS	YARDS PER RUSH	YARDS PER GAME	TOUCH-DOWNS
Atlanta Falcons	7	139	503	3.6	71.9	3
Baltimore/Indianapolis Colts	3	37	115	3.1	38.3	1
Buffalo Bills	1	39	155	4.0	155.0	1
Cincinnati Bengals	2	28	129	4.6	64.5	0
Cleveland Browns	2	33	143	4.3	71.5	1
Dallas Cowboys	6	137	692	5.1	115.3	3
Denver Broncos	6	110	611	5.6	101.8	2
Detroit Lions	25	496	1,960	4.0	78.4	10
Green Bay Packers	24	534	2,484	4.7	103.5	19
Houston Oilers	3	58	215	3.7	71.7	
Kansas City Chiefs	3	62	277	4.5	92.3	3
L.A./Oakland Raiders	5	117	441	3.8	88.2	5
L.A. Rams	9	156	646	4.1	71.8	3
Miami Dolphins	3	45	190	4.2	63.3	1
Minnesota Vikings	24	484	2,279	4.7	95.0	15
New England Patriots	3	39	151	3.9	50.3	0
New Orleans Saints	6	130	792	6.1	132.0	6
N.Y. Giants	2	33	89	2.7	44.5	0
N.Y. Jets	2	48	106	2.2	53.0	0
Philadelphia Eagles	5	125	564	4.5	112.8	1
Pittsburgh Steelers	2	43	150	3.5	75.0	1
St. Louis Cardinals	6	130	525	4.0	87.5	6
San Diego Chargers	3	76	249	3.3	83.0	2
San Francisco 49ers	8	169	792	4.7	99.0	8
Seattle Seahawks	5	100	527	5.3	105.4	3
Tampa Bay Buccaneers	20	407	1,629	4.0	81.5	12
Washington Redskins	5	63	312	5.0	62.4	3
Totals	190	3,838	16,726	4.4	88.0	110

PHOTOGRAPHS

Al Messerschmidt/Wireimage
viii, ix, 62, Back end leaf

AP/Wide World Photos
232, 239

Barbara Mandrell/Connie Payton
191

Bill Smith
EL, EP, ER, ii, 7, 26, 27, 37, 42, 43, 45, 46, 47, 50, 51, 57, 66, 67, 70, 72, 73, 76, 80, 81, 84, 90, 96, 97, 101, 102, 104, 105, 110, 111, 113, 119, 120, 123, 130, 131, 134, 135, 143, 144, 146, 148, 150, 152, 154, 156, 157, 158, 163, 166, 167, 169, 175, 195, 203, 242, 243

Bob Chwedyk
86

Bob Langer
3

Columbia, MS High School
13, 16, 19

Connie Payton
5, 8, 94, 176, 178, 180, 181, 185, 186, 187, 190, 192, 197, 200, 201, 204, 205, 206, 207, 209, 212, 218, 221, 222, 223, 224, 227, 228, 229, 230, 234, 238, Back End Leaf

Corbis
54, 55, 59, 88, 89, 99, 107, 114, 182, 183, 199, 213, 236

Don Lansu/Wireimage
161

Jackson State University
20, 23, 29, 31, 33, 34, 35, 36

Jasper Ruhe
215, 216, 217

John Biever (Favre)
x

Jonathan Daniel
61, 64, 124, 172, 173, 240, 241

Mike Lanigan
140

Paddock Publication, Inc.
210

Ron Amour
127

Tom Cruze (Payton)
x

UPI
194

Vernon Biever
3, 22, 38, 44, 53, 112, 116, 166, 188, 189

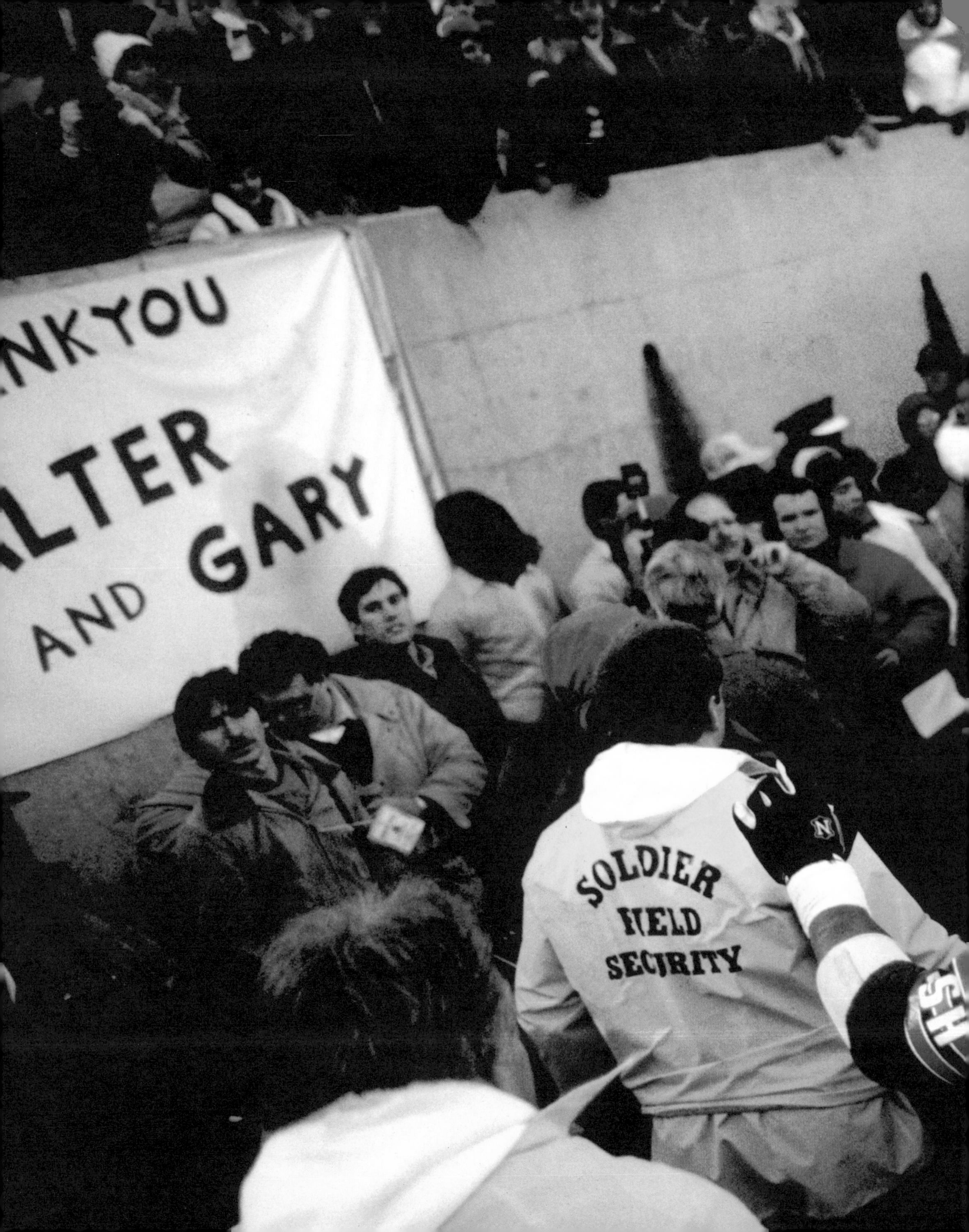
NKYOU
LTER
AND GARY
SOLDIER
FIELD
SECURITY